Introduction to Child, Adolescent, and Adult Development

A Psychoanalytic Perspective for Students and Professionals

Ivan Sherick, PhD

Ivan Sherick, PhD
220 Riverview Drive
Ann Arbor, Mi 48104
743-662-2211
isherick@umich.edu

ISBN-10: 1475078935
EAN-13: 9781475078930

Dedication

This book is dedicated to my wife, my children and their spouses, and to my grandchildren

Table Of Contents

Acknowledgments

My education began with the writings of Sigmund Freud, the founder of Psychoanalysis. His daughter, Miss Anna Freud, the founder and Director of the Hampstead Clinic in London inspired me as a student at her Clinic. Erna Furman's writing on early childhood development and Peter Blos, Sr.'s on the complexities of adolescent development have enriched me.

Numerous supervisors have assisted me and there have been many colleagues that I have discussed psychoanalytic child development with. I am grateful, also, to my supervisees and students who have challenged me to be organized and articulate in my exposition of psychoanalytic views on development. Thanks to Drs. Peter Blos, Jr., and James Heitler for reading an earlier version of this manuscript and making helpful suggestions.

My wife, Judie, has taught me a great deal about parenting. I am eternally grateful to her. Finally, my children Chaya and Dan, have given me the opportunity to be a parent and grandparent to wonderful grandchildren. I am also eternally grateful to all of them.

Introduction

My aim is to offer an introduction to the topic of development of the mind. I will consider this development over the lifetime of an individual. There will be no formal references in the text, although I will provide a list of recommended readings at the end. To help a reader relocate a subject I will provide a representative list of topics discussed in each chapter at the end. My focus is limited to the Western culture that I am familiar with. Clearly, my thinking has been formed by experiences communicated by former teachers, supervisors, colleagues, scholars, etc., to whom I am indebted, but what I offer is my own personalized synthesis of it all. The topic of the mind is so complicated that any one book cannot do justice to it.

My particular orientation is not a popular one in the present day. I am a psychoanalyst, having experience with patients of all ages. If you are in training to be a mental health specialist your program may de-emphasize a psychodynamic approach. It could be that psychoanalysis is a perspective about development of the mind that you are not familiar with. My doctorate is in clinical psychology and my internship was with adult patients. Even so, during graduate training I sought out child focused practicums. My post-doctoral training was at Reiss-Davis, a former psychoanalytically informed child guidance clinic in Los Angeles. I then completed the training in child psychoanalysis at the Hampstead Clinic in London, under Miss Anna Freud's directorship. After graduating, I completed training in adult psychoanalysis at the Michigan Psychoanalytic Institute in the USA.

I bring a developmental and ego psychological perspectives into my clinical and teaching efforts. What do these perspectives mean in simple terms? By a "developmental" perspective I mean that I do not lose sight of the continuity of a person, pulled forward by an inherent developmental force, from childhood through adulthood and into old age, as well as the timelessness of experience in the human mind. A developmental perspective looks backward and looks forward. I am interested in the interaction of the environment with an individual's maturing inherited potentialities, and the psychological and learned aspects of the mind, resulting in personal experience. Out of this interaction, the mind develops. I also attend to the psychological developmental tasks that we all must deal with at different stages of our life. While continuity is fundamental, it is not all-inclusive. Maturational changes – some physical (like puberty) and some mental (like changes in cognition) that affect ego capacities – will introduce non-linear discontinuities that can be transformative in their consequences. Also, unpredictable environmental experiences can lead to identifications and transformative outcomes.

By an "ego psychological" perspective I mean that the human mind is faced with conflicting demands, some unconscious, and expends effort to avoid mental pain and to maximize pleasure. It is this complicated, but real and valid, view of development that I hope to bring to your attention. The predominant focus will be on child and adolescent development but I extend my observations to the whole lifespan.

I hope my particular psychoanalytic perspective will be helpful to you. If you are a graduate of a psychoanalytic institute I hope you will find my views stimulating enough to further your reflection on issues about development. While there are many valuable contemporary contributions to psychoanalysis, they need to be integrated with more classical contributions. This is a task that I have not taken upon myself in this manuscript. I have, however, referred to the concepts of mentalisation and attachment insofar as I believe they are derived from our existing theory of child development and extend our understanding of the development of the mind. When considering child development, I focus mainly on the comprehensive developmental insights particularly derived from the writings of Anna Freud. In my judgment they are immensely valuable and I believe if we lose sight of them we will lose much that is helpful in working with children and parents. Currently such views, in my opinion, are neglected in the contemporary psychoanalytic literature and rarely cited. My hope is that in my introduction to these concepts I succeed in underscoring their continued usefulness. I rely on Peter Blos, Sr.'s formulations about adolescent development that also are in this tradition, as is the ego psychology perspective of psychoanalysis that I employ.

Psychoanalysis, in general, is disparaged in films and many non-psychoanalytic professionals in the field discredit it. They may discredit it but they often will take components of it into their own practices and theories without attribution as to its origin. They will say that psychoanalysis is like an extinct insect frozen in amber. The latest neuroscience evidence, however, supports much of what Freud theorized at a time when modern technology such as MRI was not available to allow electro-imaging of the brain. Additionally, empirical research underscores the efficacy of psychodynamic psychotherapeutic approaches based on psychoanalysis with patients.

What I am presenting is my personal view of a psychoanalytic perspective on development. You should know that psychoanalysis is not a unified theory and is in flux. There will be psychoanalysts who might disagree with some of what I say. I have tried to be practical and focus on the concerns most young professionals have about their patients and those brought by parents in consultations about their children and about their parenting. The stages of adulthood will also be considered from becoming a parent to old age.

I will try in what follows to introduce you to how this particular psychoanalyst views development in language that is intelligible. When technical concepts are used I will explain them in language that is more comprehensible but still able to convey the nuances and complexity of the concept. My purpose in including theory about a model of the mind and about psychological conflict is to help you understand how an analyst conceptualizes the workings of the mind. My hope is that it will allow you to appreciate not only your patient's mind, but also your own. Having a theory is like providing you with a flashlight as you enter a dark cave in which are the most extraordinary paintings and carvings created by ancient people. The theory can help you to know what to look for and how to understand what you see. Development is complex, so rarely do simplistic linear formulations suffice as causative explanations. Instead, we think of outcomes as usually being multi-determined.

For the most part, I am focusing on normal development but will diverge my focus to "psychopathology" when I think it might be helpful. As a psychoanalyst, when I think of "normal" I am not thinking of ordinary or conventional or obedient. Insofar as mental conflict is ubiquitous, the normal individual is also " normally neurotic." "Neurotic" for a psychoanalyst is not a pejorative term. All of us, to a lesser or greater degree, are neurotic.

The book is organized in a description of stages of development that roughly follows chronological age. These stages of development are characterized by familiar epochs in the lives of people, e.g., newborn, toddler, preschooler, school age, middle school student, teenager, young adult, middle age, grandparent, and old age. These stages also inter-relate with "phases" of development that psychoanalysts distinguish by the kinds of personal issues and conflicts characteristic for that particular period of development. I will relate a descriptive stage and corresponding psychoanalytic phase to one another in non-technical terms. Interspersed will be a variety of topics that concern professionals insofar as they impinge upon a child's development, e.g., divorce. I have tried to address these topics at the stage of development when parents usually consider them, but in real life it is not so orderly and predictable.

Often I will refer to parental attitudes and concerns insofar when discussing a child's development it is impossible to do so without considering parents. There are no children without parents (adult caregivers). Almost all children develop in the context of a family. The parenting skills of mothers and fathers, or lack of them, have major consequences for a child's development. As a professional dealing with children you will need to deal with their parents. You will be asked to give parental guidance. Sometimes an interpretation to a parent about their parenting will be a timely intervention. If you work only with adults, your patients will recount memories of interactions with their parents. Your knowledge of child development and parenting issues can inform your work with adults and be helpful to you as a psychodynamic therapist or psychoanalyst.

The book is divided up into three parts. Part 1 involves what we call childhood and adolescence. The second, Part 2, involves the young adult years through old age. Part 3 has to do with obtaining professional help. I hope you find in these pages something of value to help you understand your patients whatever his or her age. I include a list of topics discussed in each chapter as a guide to the contents of the book. I conclude with a section of recommended readings.

PART 1

Chapter 1
The Decision To Have A Child

Partners can benefit from taking the time to know each other better in an intimate relationship without the added responsibilities of attending to a newborn. A true partnership can evolve with each member feeling equity has been achieved. Issues of career, life style, avocational pursuits, etc., can be consolidated more or less by young adults who have committed themselves to each other and are ready to consider parenthood as a new stage of being adult. Thus, entering parenthood does not depend solely on giving birth to an infant but entails a mental change in how you view yourself, your partner, and a child you will care for, as well as the relationships between the three of you.

It makes intuitive sense to me that a couple does not rush into parenthood. Parenthood can be postponed these days with aware- ness and availability of birth control measures. Of course, postponing the decision, beginning with the current practice of getting married later in age, can introduce issues of infertility that seem more frequent in contemporary times than in the past. Issues of infertility, adoption, and couples of the same gender becoming parents, are increasingly present and I will devote a chapter to them later on.

Once conception occurs it will not be "business as usual." The future mother needs to attend to the specific health needs of her new pregnant state. She will find herself increasingly imagining, first, the fetus growing within her own self-boundaries, and, second, as a being outside of her. But it will take a period of time, if ever in some cases, that the child-to-be will be felt to be a separate and autonomous per- son outside of her own personal boundaries. A first-time mother may find herself worried about the well being of her fetus and will need the support of her spouse.

For some men, their wives' increasing preoccupation with the unborn baby may feel threatening, and they may feel rivalrous with the unborn baby. If he recognizes this he may feel embarrassed or even guilty. The expectant father may have doubts about his capacity to be an economic provider, the traditional role of males. If they cannot talk openly about this to their wife, perhaps they can to a male friend.

Some expectant fathers can be envious of their pregnant partners. It is rare, but sometimes men have simulated symptoms of being pregnant, e.g., experiencing morning sickness or weight gain. This virtual pregnancy is known as "couvade." Most men are unaware of the link to their wife's pregnancy. Those who recognize the connection may not want to speak openly about such thoughts but it would be helpful to them if they could. They may feel ashamed or embarrassed, believing such thoughts and feelings not to be masculine.

Together the couple will need to prepare the "nest," the nursery area for the yet to be born baby. Family and friends will need to be told about the expected baby, and the choice of a name will be considered. What would seem to be matter-of-fact actions can, for some couples, become stressors. For example, rivalries with siblings, dealing with too intrusive or indifferent future grandparents, and extended family expectations about names can complicate what ordinarily is a time of happiness and increased feelings of self worth.

Likely, the motive to become a parent has a biological, evolutionary component. The survival of the species depends upon it. The early doll play of young girls supports a proposition of an inborn tendency to parent. Likely, some of this play will be the young girl's doing with her dolls what her mother did with her. It's hard for a male to empathize with a pregnant woman but not impossible. The feeling of being fertile and nurturing a new future person that will grow inside of you, must be a powerful motive to become a parent. For the male to feel he has contributed to this, must allow for a similar feeling of creativity. To express a generative need is part of the stage of parenthood. A derivative of this generative need, an attitude that is consolidated in the young adult, is being creative in life and the sense of being productive in a career. Presumably, for some young adults, the idea of nurturing a child and exposing them to ideals that could allow them to mature into individuals that a parent could feel proud of, serves as a motive.

A wish to be like one's own parent likely plays a role in the decision to try to conceive. This wish to use one's own same-gendered parent as a model, if realized, results in a modification of the mind's image of one's self. The result of such an identification is sort of an unconscious expansion of one's self image. Identifications are not necessarily intentional, nor always adaptive. A boy who is scared of his harsh unaffectionate father could identify with him and act the same way in the future when he becomes a father. You can see how intergenerational problems can get transmitted. Identifications, however, need not be based only upon fear, but can also be based on emulation, e.g., admiring a nurturing father, so our boy grows up to be one too.

In some instances there may be less noble aims, likely unconscious ones that motivate becoming a parent. A potential mother or father may have unmet goals in their life and may unwittingly aspire for their unborn children to accomplish what they could not so they can have vicarious pleasure. Often this motive can have an invidious outcome because the child's uniqueness regarding talents and interests is ignored. The result is disappointment for all concerned.

It is difficult for a young adult to get their mind around issues of mortality, but such concerns are ubiquitous, albeit kept out of consciousness for many. A child carrying your DNA that looks like you allows for an illusion of immortality. In some instances, a couple may unwittingly conceive to distract themselves from a failing marriage and with the hope of rescuing it. Fortunately, most children are conceived with the best of intentions and are welcomed into an orbit of love and future promise.

As parents enter parenthood, they best not to think of it in an idealized manner. Being a "good" parent is not being a "perfect" parent. Perfection is a fiction when it comes to the complicated job of parenting. Good parents do not succeed in making their child invulnerable to life's trials and tribulations. I am fond of the Greek myth of

Achilles. Recall how his mother dipped him in some magical water to make him invincible. To do this she needed to hold him by one ankle lest he drown, this area of his body remaining vulnerable and the eventual site of a fatal injury. It is impossible to shield children from every untoward experience. Becoming a "good enough" parent means facilitating children to become self-reliant and self-fulfilled within their own potential. This way they will do their best with untoward events and develop personal resilience.

Let me address the issue of co-parenting between spouses. Certainly men are more involved in direct childcare than they were two generations earlier. They change diapers, they participate in bottle feedings, they may be the one who responds to the nighttime distress calls of their child, etc. Likely, this is a response to feminism which enabled men to re-evaluate masculinity. Men discovered that nurturance and masculinity are compatible.

Chapter 2
A New-Born & First-Time-Parenting/Oral Phase

Have you noticed new parents gazing at their baby? From the expression on their faces you can surmise that they are in wonder that the adorable being is their child. He or she looks like them and/or the partner. They notice the beautiful hands and feet and a wonderful complexion. A baby will bring parents much pleasure but also being a parent will be a challenge.

One of the first questions parents might ask you, as an expert, is should the baby sleep in the parental bedroom in the parental bed or a separate bed, or in a separate bedroom? I know that having the family sleep together in one bed has been gaining in popularity in recent years. I, however, do not advise it, mainly for two reasons. The first is based on safety. I would be concerned all night about inadvertently rolling over onto the infant and suffocating it. Secondly, the issue of privacy would be a concern, especially as the infant gets older. Privacy issues would apply to both instances, either where the baby sleeps in the parental bed or in a separate bed in the parents' bedroom. Spouses usually seek resuming sexual intimacy soon after childbirth and the presence of the infant in the bed could make this burdensome. As the child gets older, excluding him or her would be based on the rationale that witnessing the parents engaging in sex will be over-stimulating and not beneficial to the child.

Having the infant in a nearby room of its own makes sense because the child and mother will need to accommodate themselves to becoming physically separate from each other. Often parents will choose expediency in deciding where to have the infant sleep. After all, night time feedings will be more easily achieved if the baby is physically present and sleep will be less disturbed if you only have to roll over to feed. Expediency, however, is usually never the correct choice in parenting. Taking the time even if inconvenient always turns out to be prudent.

Infants will benefit for their entire lives if they learn how to soothe themselves. Sleeping in the parental bed makes this less likely to occur. Infants who find a finger to suck or a soft doll or blanket to handle are being masterful and adaptive. In the long run, their tolerance for frustration will benefit. This is the ability to tolerate an unmet need for increasing durations of time. They will be able to calm themselves sufficiently until the mother appears. They will be able to put themselves to sleep. Later on it will not be necessary for a parent to be in bed with them until they fall asleep or to introduce extreme measures like taking them for a ride in a car to induce sleeping. The thumb to suck becomes a substitute for the nipple and the sucking satisfies the non-nutritional component of sucking, providing pleasure for the so-called oral needs of the infant (more about this later).

A valued soft doll or blanket in the crib has been termed a "transitional object" insofar as it is thought to represent in the mind of the baby aspects of him or herself and also of the major care-giving person they are involved with, usually the mother. It is as if the thing valued represents a transition from a focus for gratification on the self and internal world to the external world. For example, the scent may contain remnants of mother's perfume as well as scents from the baby's own saliva. The satin edge of the blanket may feel like mother's skin. A child will rub the satin edge on their cheek or will finger it, behaviors reminiscent of nursing at the breast. A transitional object usually does not appear to be valued by the baby until around at least six months, a point in the child's life that he or she is sorting out what sensations and perceptions are part of them and which are part of the surround. Some parents have difficulties with their baby having a transitional object insofar as they want their child to be soothed by them and not by an inanimate object or part of the baby's own body such as a thumb. It is best for parents not to remove a transitional object by hiding or throwing it away as this will be very upsetting to the baby. The transitional object usually fades away in importance as the child grows older.

It is always difficult for parents to know at what point they should intervene when their infant is crying. After all, the newborn seems so helpless. There are no hard and fast rules here, insofar as each parent's tolerance differs as does each baby's. But there are some guidelines. First, a baby will not die from crying which likely is an unconscious primordial fear of a parent. Recall that the aim is for the infant to learn to console itself. If a parent is too quick to intervene one cannot expect a baby to attain self-consoling behaviors. My sense is that through trial and error parents will learn their child's threshold for becoming inconsolable. Parents need to pick up their children and assist them to become consoled. Intuitively, a parent will lengthen the period of delay of intervention, as the child gets older and more capable of tolerating frustration and being self-soothing.

Spouses need to support each other during these early days of parenthood, especially first-time parents. One should keep in mind that there is a learning curve for new parents and most will become competent for the task. A grandmother, sibling, or friend who has been through it can be a mentor.

Some infants are prone to a digestive distress known as colic. It starts in some infants from birth and lasts often until three months of age, but for some infants it is extended in duration. Infants experiencing colic are often crying and appear to be inconsolable. It sometimes helps if a parent holds them in an upright position, so their eyes are open, swaddled, and firmly against your own body. But for some infants nothing seems to calm them. Some parents, in a frantic effort to calm them and to help them sleep will put babies in an infant bed secured in an automobile and drive around the neighborhood. The motion of the moving car seems to help. It's easy to feel incompetent when your baby seems inconsolable despite your best efforts. Parents need to be aware that the cause of colic is not their responsibility. This is one condition that infants truly "grow out of." Spouses need to support one another during such times.

The choice to nurse or bottle-feed needs to be made. It is likely the choice was made before the birth. It is important that mothers not be made to feel guilty by others if they choose contrary to what is thought to be better. Besides the obvious nutritional needs that a mother must satisfy, consideration is also paid to the mode that will best satisfy the need for intimacy for a nursing couple. Whether nursing or bottle-feeding, this is an opportunity for mother and baby to gaze into each other's eyes and to establish a unique bond or attachment. Intuitively, most caregivers will treat these occasions as special, not an opportunity to speak on the phone or watch television.

This bonding is the foundation for empathy, for sensing what another separate individual is feeling, and facilitates coming in touch with what you, yourself, are feeling. Recent research suggests "mirror neurons" in primates like monkeys. If so, they may also be discovered in humans. Essentially, this means that the same area of the brain is activated when two primates are interacting in an involved emotional manner. It is as if the brain constructs an experience of the other person in the same part of the brain for the same self-experience. Presumably this neurological event underlies empathy. A corollary of this is that we infer that as the newborn ages, he or she feels "emotionally held" when his or her mother is emotionally attuned with it. This emotional attunement is an important foundational requirement for the developing sense of self. When a mother "mirrors" her infant she is helping the child process feelings. She essentially mimics the infant's feelings on her own face or with a vocalization that conveys an understanding to the infant of their own feelings. In this way we speak of the infant's mental self or space as expanding.

If one observes a nursing mother and her baby, one cannot but be impressed with the sense of reciprocity that includes pleasure and intimacy. Out of this physical experience is the birth of a psychological experience, the beginning of a sense of self and eventually of "other." If the infant places its finger in mother's mouth perhaps we are seeing the origin of play?

From birth to approximately the first two years of life the infant is developmentally engaged in the so-called "oral phase." Please keep in mind that when I give approximate ages when phases appear that individual differences results in some variation, and that phases overlap, i.e. one phase may begin when another is still present. One particular phase is the most influential or dominant in the mind of the child during a particular time period.

Let us return to the oral phase. What this means is that inborn physiological needs exist that become psychophysiological when they make specific demands to be satisfied upon the immature mind of the infant. When these needs go unsatisfied the infant experiences frustration and in reaction to this unpleasant feeling, anger. It is satisfying to suck and by the time teeth appear, to bite. If either of these component oral needs, during many instances, is either frustrated or gratified too much, derivative oral behaviors or oral personality features can become permanent characteristics or signature traits of the person. What is "too much" deprivation or gratification will differ for each person, likely based upon inborn biological factors such as the "strength" of an instinct (need). Most of us have some "permanent" derivative features from each phase of development, based upon multiple determinants.

Please keep in mind that personality traits are formed by multiple determinants. Personality features of being overly pessimistic or optimistic may have as one contribution, respectively, deprivation or over-gratification of the first part of the oral phase (sucking). Examples derived from the later biting stage of the oral phase would be sarcasm (deprivation) and being tenacious (over-gratification). We all know adults who portray such features as characteristics of their personalities.

Healthy derivatives also appear in adult lovemaking, e.g., as part of foreplay (kissing, sucking and gentle biting). Such observations and the psychoanalyses of adults suggest that pleasure from sucking and biting is sexual in quality. Biting also satisfies an aggressive urge. At this early age both sexual and aggressive urges are intertwined. If you have ever seen a toddler express a loving feeling towards a newborn, a kitten, or puppy, you know you have to be there to supervise lest the toddler can hurt the recipient of their affection.

The aim of an urge can be either active and/or passive. If active, the aim is to act upon another; if passive, the aim is to be acted upon by another. An example might be to bite (active) or to be bitten (passive). When both active and passive aims co-exist, we call this conflict ambivalence. One side of this conflict within the mind likely will be unconscious. This type of ambivalence is hard for us to intuit. Our evidence is based on the clinical psychoanalyses of people of all ages, and on our understanding of fairytales that express such universal themes. The fairytale "Little Red Riding Hood" is relevant for the oral dynamics we are examining. A child's behavior, both interactive with you or privately within their own mind, may be examples of these dynamics. A young child may wish to bite you and even express a wish that you try to bite them, like two kittens at play. Or the child may want to take turns being a wolf that is trying to blow a house down to catch the occupants and eat them.

Let us consider thumb sucking. It usually starts around two to three months of age in a consistent way. Not all children do suck their thumb. It is a natural way for the baby to satisfy the psychophysiological need to suck. It is a way for the infant to soothe itself when frustrated or falling asleep. During the activity of thumb sucking, part of one's own body satisfies and brings erotic pleasure to a sexually sensitive area of the body, the oral cavity. Thumb sucking bothers many parents. They prefer that they soothe the baby. For others there is concern about future orthodontic needs and expenses. Most importantly, the baby should not be shamed or scolded for thumb sucking. Many babies that choose to thumb suck reduce their interest in this activity once they progress into the next phase of instinctual drive expression. Some children will persist for a long time (into the fourth year) because of an oral fixation and they or their parents may need professional help. In a later chapter I will discuss what I mean by a "fixation." Introducing a pacifier does not allow an infant to discover its own method of self-soothing.

During these early months, children will become increasingly aware of themselves and of the world. They will benefit from all their senses, gradually building up in their mind an internal representation of the animate and inanimate world. We now know that newborns are more capable of seeing and hearing the world, than we thought, from day one. Newborns are able to distinguish intonational sounds from each parent's language from each other and from the language of others. Hearing mother's sounds helps with affect regulation. The child looks at things that mother points to, gradually building up a group of external referents in connection with their particular relationship. The child who looks does not look at itself, the looker, but the child who speaks hears itself, the speaker. Hence, seeing likely objectifies while speaking and hearing involves intrasubjectivity. These two senses help build up an "object" (an "other") and a "self." (In psychoanalysis we call the person one loves or hates an "object" to distinguish the person from the self, the "subject." It is not meant to dehumanize a person.) Infants do not recognize themselves in a mirror until the second year.

It is via the mouth that much of the world is first experienced by the newborn. Everything seems to end up in the infant's mouth. Eventually the fingers enter the mouth and they will help the baby to explore. The child's hand will be very important in helping to distinguish oneself from non-self. At first, the hand is likely a thing like other things that are seen and felt. It is only with one's own body as a thing, however, that the infant can simultaneously experience both touching and being touched. Delay of gratification will also aid the infant to distinguish between self and the environment. If gratification is not immediate it must be coming from "out there." With time, a particular "other", the mother, or caregiver becomes a psychic image. Gradually, the boundaries of the body will consolidate and a rudimentary body image will be established by the end of the first year. Many experiences of gratification and frustration will contribute to a differentiation between a remembered gratification, a memory, and an actual gratification, a perception.

Between the second and third month the baby will reliably smile at the sight of significant caregivers. I say "reliably" smile because you will likely see evidence of smiling earlier but you cannot be confident that it is meant to be a social awareness response and not a reaction to an intestinal stimulus. Nothing gives parents more pleasure than the smile of their baby in response to their own smile. Perhaps second to this pleasure is the time the baby first says a "word" like "Ma" or "Da." This usually occurs around the sixth month. Also, other milestones are sitting up (around six months), standing up (around ten-twelve months), and the first step (around ten-twelve months).

It is important to keep in mind that each child is different and the chronological age when behaviors first appear will differ, so that parental worry that a child is abnormal in almost all instances is unnecessary. If the delay is very significant a pediatrician will bring it to a parent's attention. Parents differ as to which behaviors they reinforce and it is likely these will progress at a more rapid rate than others. In some instances a behavior may develop in a precocious manner. For example, if parents are particularly invested in language they will make a bigger deal out of the child's utterances while more athletically inclined parents might reinforce signs of motoric agility. In any case, most children grow up to be "well rounded" individuals having the basic equipment to benefit from educational and other kinds of experience.

It is very important to understand that a parent's psychic reality, the subjective internal image of one's child, **is** the objective reality that impinges upon the child and to which he or she must accommodate. It is, as if, an unconscious image is treated as equivalent to a perception. For example, if a parent continually imposes an image of their own sibling upon that of their child, the child may grow up and have personality characteristics like the parent's sibling. A child's personality can become a self-fulfilling prophecy. Another way to say this is that expectations we have of a child influences how we react to that child, as well as effecting how the child feels about itself and behaves. A parent can exaggerate strengths and/or weaknesses of a child. The less objective is the view of one's child the more likely problems can arise.

A baby will benefit from routines. Children thrive on routines and become disrupted by the unpredictable. This is not to say that spontaneity is bad. The showing of affection is always beneficial and cannot be scheduled. But eating and bedtime, for example, are the kind of routines that are helpful to schedule. When babies build up expectations and these prove true it contributes to a trustful sense of the world as predictable and gratifying. The child's sense of reality and reality testing are enhanced. Reality testing establishes a concept of cause and effect and later helps in making choices. Recognition of the principle of cause and effect also underlies rational thinking. I hope I am conveying to you that the future development of a child can benefit from a firm foundation.

This topic leads me to digress for a moment and talk about issues more pertinent to an older child. I hope this digression further helps you to see the continuity of development and the importance of looking to the past to help understand the present and the future child. Older children need to be given appropriate choices. Choices are best when limited and succinct. For example, they can choose doing their homework either before or after bathing. Threats should not be made and are unnecessary if the choices are appropriate. Choices are presented positively, not negatively. A negative choice would be to say if they do not do their homework they will not be allowed to watch television. This wrongly focuses on watching television. A child could elect not to do their homework and forgo watching television. Establishing limits enters here insofar as children learn natural consequences have a connection to their choices. Thus, if they bathe and want to watch television but have not finished their homework a natural consequence will be that they will not be able to.

Paying careful attention to limits early on in the child's life will have important implications down the road. If limits were allowed to be disregarded from the beginning, one cannot introduce them later on and expect the misbehaving older child to give them any credence. When no limits are set, children become scared of their own powers. Their parents are the ones they depend upon to protect them from their own powerful urges and if parents fail them in this manner, children get anxious. Parents need to learn the difference between discipline and punishment.

Discipline is when the parental aim is to help the child establish internal regulations to help control intense feelings and focus on the desired outcome. This usually involves talking to the child and processing the sequence of events of which the parent is disapproving. A good criterion for setting limits is always safety of the child, not arbitrary ones established to underscore the authority of the parent. But what is the consequence to the child of their misbehaving? A natural consequence is parental disapproval. Children want very much to be approved of by parents. Not to be approved of diminishes their security and as they get older results in guilt. We distinguish between healthy guilt and neurotic guilt. It is appropriate for the older child to be motivated by healthy guilt when they do not live up to reasonable parental standards of behavior, and later internalized standards.

Neurotic guilt could involve feeling contrite for something imagined but not committed.

The aim is not to instill guilt but to help the child internalize a moral compass to help them regulate intense feelings and imperative urges. With very young children, of course, processing the errant behavior often cannot occur verbally. We must keep in mind, however, that even young children have receptive language comprehension before they have expressive language. That is, they can understand long before they can make themselves understood. A stern "No" will suffice for the very young. Parents best aim to communicate clearly to children, regardless of their age, that it is the behavior you disapprove of, not them as a person, whom you love. Sometimes a consequence for older children may need to be the withholding of a privilege that they have abused. For example, withholding computer time if the child has spent more than the agreed upon time on it the day before. I rarely see the sense in "time outs" when young children are sent to their room for misbehaving. First of all, the physical separation can create anxiety for some children. Also, the parental expectation that the child will "think" about what happened likely only rarely takes place. Instead the child angrily distracts him or herself. Having the child sit quietly within sight of the parent makes more sense. I will discuss neurotic guilt later.

When parents punish a child for a transgression they are expressing their anger and disappointment towards their child and wish to hurt the child. Usually, they feel their authority as an adult and parent has been disregarded and this evokes anger. The angry parent often chooses a consequence that has no connection to the child's transgression. As a parent, we feel guilty to recognize our anger towards our child whom we love. I think it is very important that parents accept that they can harbor an angry wish towards a loved child. I say this early in this exposition and emphatically because unless parents can accept and acknowledge this they will have difficulties in setting limits. They will have trouble distinguishing limits from an angry expression. They will also feel they are "bad" and feel relentlessly guilty. They may react by being extremely "nice" to the child. Every parent is capable of being physically abusive or even sadistic towards one of his or her children. I say this because in the unconscious part of the mind, even something as horrific as an infanticidal fantasy may reside. But there is a **world of difference** between having a wish or fantasy and enacting it. Hopefully, it is the exception and not the rule that parents enact their anger physically. Of course, even a rare instance is once too many. More likely, parents use their words to shame or humiliate a child towards whom they are angry. This, too, is unnecessary and can be injurious to a child's psyche.

Let me return to our infant. From birth, infants demonstrate intense feelings. Likely some feelings are inborn so that there is a readiness for the feeling to be manifested if the releasing stimulus is present, e.g., a loud noise will cause a startle. From birth onward the infant gradually learns to regulate feelings with the help of his caregivers. Parents gradually learn to discriminate the meaning of different distress cries their infants' present. One cry may mean hunger (thirst), another pain, and yet another feeling cold. With experience, a mother will learn that when her infant appears to be angry it could be that he is really distressed about something that is not being effectively communicated to the infant. In the first few years of life, children have few words to convey how they feel. Hence, they may say they "hate" when a better descriptor might be " don't like." By helping children label their feelings parents help them become better communicators and regulators of their feelings. This labeling of feelings by parents begins in the first year of life. You can observe mothers intuiting the feelings behind their infants' expressions and offering names to them.

During these early months a gradual differentiation will occur between mother and her newborn. Mother's self-boundaries which once included the baby growing inside of her, must now allow for the baby to be separate and outside of her own self. For mothers the unity at first was both biological and psychological. Intellectually, mothers know this but emotionally this takes time and mothers differ as to how long. For the child there is the same evolution but it's beginning was biological. We presume that awareness of the mother is at first based entirely on need satisfaction and only gradually evolves into a psychological connection. We then speak of a social awareness. The awareness of mother, the "other," we presume is initially based on "parts" of her, e.g., the rhythm and timbre of her voice, the quality of her touch, her scent, her smile, the sound of her gait, etc. We call these self-other moment's "part object" experiences. Later, they will be experienced as "transitional phenomena" (see below). With repeated such part object experiences a whole object experience is built up, probably towards the end of the second year. The child's sense of self apart from its caregiver is a gradual process.

As indicated above, much of it occurs in the context of inter-actions with its caregiver, in most instances its mother. There are countless interactions of caring involving feeding, bathing, dressing, playing, cuddling, reflections about feelings, etc., wherein the mother serves as a "mirror" for the child. We will talk more about this later in Chapter 5 when we speak of mentalization. I do not mean to sound mystical, but it is in mother's gentle touch, the lilt of her voice, the smile in her eyes, and other demonstrations of responsiveness that contribute to the infant's sense that itself is an entity, or being. Also, the bodily experiences and perceptions of its own body, mentioned earlier, as well as interactions with the rest of the world contribute to the infant's emerging sense of identity, of differentiation out of an undifferentiated state of being. While a differentiation is occurring, a parallel process of "being with" is also ongoing. The infant gradu-ally feels an attachment to the caregiver. An essential aspect of the developing attachment being an emotional attunement of the infant's feelings to those of the maternal object conveyed via her touch, voice and facial expression.

Mention should be made of postpartum depression that affects a minority of women. The time of onset varies after the birth of the newborn. Mothers feel depressed or sad, easily given to cry-ing without apparent cause. This condition is likely caused by the hormonal changes during pregnancy and is usually short-lived. After some weeks or a couple of months it seems to pass and the mother feels more like her usual self. Because of these feelings, some of these women feel guilty because they believe they have not been as attentive to their infant as they would have liked. This maternal guilt might be considered healthy insofar as the mother has not been able to function as effectively as she hoped even if not responsible, and it motivates her to be responsive once again to her child. If the guilt is severe and long lasting then it is no longer healthy. A spouse can be very helpful by being supportive and stepping in to give their partner respite during this trying time.

Chapter 3
Infertility, Multiples, & Adoption

Infertility

Infertility can be an insufferable experience for some couples that have made the decision to become parents. A sense of inadequacy and failure can diminish feelings of self-worth. An infertile couple finds it difficult to be around friends or family that have children and who ask about their intentions to become parents. Fortunately, modern science and medicine can be of help with techniques to maximize chances of fertility or to artificially cause insemination by laboratory means. This is expensive and most often not covered by medical insurance. Those who have the financial means are fortunate.

There are different arrangements, e.g., the eggs may be harvested from the female of the couple or from a surrogate and similarly with the sperm. the egg can be fertilized *in vitro* in a laboratory or via intra-uterine insemination. The fertilized egg then can be implanted in the female partner or in a surrogate mother. Or intra-uterine insemination can take place, if possible. Of course, regardless of the arrangements there will be intense feelings. Even if it is each partner's own egg and sperm there will be regrets that conception did not occur naturally. But at least in this case, one can be reassured that the child is your "own" with your DNA. Nevertheless, an infertile partner must deal with the fact that a surrogate was necessary. It's not inevitable that this has to become a major issue for the infertile member of the couple. It will, however, be a reality about which each parent will have feelings. It is better to talk openly about these feelings with a partner than to suppress them.

What do parents tell children conceived unnaturally when they are older and inevitably ask questions about their birth? Professionals do not have sufficient experience yet with this population to be of much help with guidance. My own sense is to tell the truth about the conception. This would be told in the context of how important it was to become a parent and how sought after the child was. If there was a surrogate involved either as a donor or carrier of the fertilized egg, my inclination is to delay imparting this information until the child is older, e.g., at least until 8 years of age and preferably until adolescence. My reason for this has the same rationale as delaying the facts of adoption, if possible, until the child is older, which I will discuss later in this chapter. I do think that a parent should elevate a donor sperm or egg to the status, respectively, of a biological father or biological mother, when talking to a child. Intuitively, I assume this would help children, if inclined, to fantasize about their biological parent. It is through such mental processing that a child will be able to integrate the facts of their conception.

A word about miscarriages is in order. How to treat a woman who has miscarried a pregnancy has changed the last twenty years. My impression is that prior to that time, professionals did not give it the consideration that it is due. It was believed to be a disappointment but not a significant loss for a woman. We know better now. It is imperative that spouses, relatives and friends not trivialize the loss. A prospective mother that miscarries needs to be allowed to mourn her unborn child. Every pregnant woman has fantasies of the unborn child and these will need to be mourned as well. A memorial service of some kind is recommended by some professionals to assist in the process. A woman who miscarries may irrationally blame herself and feel guilty. One young mother, already caring for a toddler, felt relieved after the miscarriage because she realized with hindsight that she was unprepared for a second child. But the relief in its wake brought feelings of guilt thinking of the miscarried "baby."

A woman, who miscarries, along with her spouse, is often encouraged by others to get pregnant again as soon as possible. I think this is best delayed until sufficient mourning for the miscarried fetus has occurred. Often a new child is conceived or adopted to replace a child that was born, lived awhile and then dies. If there is a rush to get pregnant again, the possibility of the new baby to become a so-called "replacement child" exists. A replacement child is at risk insofar as the identity they adopt likely will be that of the fantasized unborn child or of the child that died. Parents that have insufficiently mourned unconsciously encourage the assignment of this identity. The replacement child can grow up with an inauthentic self-identity that is not a firm foundation for dealing with the world. A replacement child may feel unattached to his or her self. Essentially, the child is being asked to identify with a dead child in order to feel alive. Of course, this is an impossible task. If a mother has not sufficiently mourned, the intense grief experienced will interfere with her ability to bond with her newborn child. It is impossible to imagine the grief experienced when a child dies. It is difficult to put an exact duration on what is "sufficient mourning," because it is so individual, but I would think in the range of six months to one year. Sometimes, parents adopt a child to be a replacement and the same concerns apply here, too.

A premature birth is another particularly stressful time for parents. There is the loss of a fantasy of a full term birth. The new mother may feel reactively depressed that she has not been able like other women to carry her baby for the full gestation period. The experience may cause her to feel diminished in some way. She irrationally may wonder if she is "less than a full women," or good mother. Also, the neonate may need to be put in an incubator for a period of time so that the mother will be unable to hold her newborn causing her to feel deprived of this basic need. If a premature infant needs to be incubated, arrangements usually can be made in most neonatal ICUs for a parent to visit and to talk and even touch or encourage sucking and feeding of the baby. Such interventions can foster a developmental attachment for both baby and mother. A healthy attachment facilitates developmental progress. If the infant is very premature its health or even survival will be uncertain and worries about it succumbing may exist. Parents will need to be very supportive of each other during this trying period until the baby is "out of the woods."

Multiples

As a result of artificial insemination, births of multiples are becoming more frequent. This results from the implanting of more than one fertilized egg in the uterus to insure success. Parents may elect not to reduce the number of implanted eggs for different reasons. The ordeal of the process following months or years of infertility may be a determinant to "get it over with," or there may be religious objections to a reduction. This is so even though they know intellectually that reducing will benefit the viability of the remaining implanted fertilized eggs. Reduction to these parents will feel the same as an objectionable abortion.

Professionals have had experiences with multiple births prior to the introduction of artificial insemination. Our experience, however, usually does not go beyond triplets. Twins are not that uncommon, while triplets are infrequent naturally. There is the possibility of identical or fraternal twins or triplets. "Sororial" is a contemporary term denoting multiple births of non-identical girls. When the twins or triplets are identical there are many psychological challenges. Individuality needs to be contended with. At a deeper level, one's sense of identity needs to be forged. Who am I? What is my essence? What makes me unique? After all, there is another person who not only resembles you, as a sibling might, but is identical to you. Only a few people can tell you apart. Some identical twins relish this and conspiratorially play games with people pretending to be the other twin. Presumably there is a sense of power that they experience. Other identical twins hate the fact that he or she is not unique and mistaken all the time for his or her twin. Fraternal or sororial twins need not deal with this. They must deal with sharing the limelight on birthdays. Competitiveness and cooperation struggle with each other. The competition might even extend to who was born "first." There is the close bond that is possible between twins or triplets that potentially brings a lifetime of companionship and support. Sometimes, being separated from the twin can be difficult. Sleeping arrangements may need to consider this. Twins may insist upon sleeping in the same room.

I need to digress here and speak about a tragic event, the death of a child. This topic, of course, can be introduced at any age in an exposition of development. An ultimate loss for an identical twin can be the death of the other twin; it can be experienced as the death of a part of one's self. Of course, the age of the surviving twin will determine the manner in which parents help the survivor cope with the loss. If the death occurs during childbirth, parents may believe the surviving twin need not be told of this happening and keep it a secret. We know from experience that family secrets (see below) are "malignant" and that it is better to talk about them when it is believed a child can comprehend the content and associated feelings and process them.

The death of a child is a terrible tragedy for parents, regardless of the age of the child. Parents need to allow themselves to mourn. During this period of grieving they will be internally focused and have difficulties attending to the external world. If there are other children, especially young ones, or newborns in the case of a surviving twin, this will be a hardship for the children. If the surviving children are older, they, too, will be dealing with a loss. In addition, they will be dealing with the temporary "loss" of their grieving parents. This is a time when relatives and friends can be especially helpful to step in and be surrogate parents. Sometimes professional help may be needed to help a family deal with a death of a child.

It is frequently observed that twins will complement one another in skills. One twin may be gregarious while the other is reticent. The reticent one may be academically advanced while the other is average, and so on. I doubt that this is consciously decided upon but is unconsciously negotiated by the twins over years of interactions. It is as if there is "unconscious" communication between the twins. This communication is based on empathy and familiarity with each other's feelings and inclinations. Analogous is how long-timed married spouses often end each other's sentences or use excessive pronouns insofar as they anticipate what is being said and who is being talked about.

Parents of twins or triplets have to deal with the practical problems of providing care for more than one child simultaneously. The greater the number of multiples, the more difficult the task. Imagine feeding triplet newborns, all of which could be thirsty or hungry at the same time. The participation of the father is essential and grandparents can also lend a hand. The early infancy period presents a strain, but there are others as the children mature. The financial costs with multiples are more than with a singleton and this can be a burden. When twins or triplets are identical, parents must decide whether or not to maximize this or minimize this. They can dress them alike or differently, part their hair on the same or different sides, etc. Then once school starts do parents lobby to have them in the same or different classes? Parents might consider allowing the twins or triplets to decide this issue, or participate in the decision-making. They may elect to start out in the same class but later revise this decision as they make separate friends.

Adoption

Adoption is not an easy decision for most couples. For those who adopt for ideological reasons it is easier. One is motivated by humanistic ideals to provide a family for an orphan or hard-to-adopt child. When the motive originates because of infertility it is more complicated. The infertile couple must deal with their infertility, as discussed earlier, and with the common fantasy that they are taking away or even stealing someone else's child, albeit an irrational fantasy. The child may have become adoptable because it was born to a single mother. The adoptive mother (or parents) may attribute, unconsciously, the "bad" behavior of the biological mother to the baby, who is then thought of as the "bad seed" of a sinful (unmarried) or delinquent mother.

Older children who are adopted may have trouble bonding with their adoptive parents and are at risk if this cannot be accomplished. They may have bonded already with a surrogate or foster caregiver and this will be broken because of the adoption. The child may react with anger towards the adoptive parents who are perceived to be the cause of the loss. If the adoptive couple has biological children, there will likely be feelings that need to be attended to by the parents. Biological children may wonder why their presence was not sufficient to satisfy their parents. While adoption can be difficult, for reasons like the above, often it can be successful and bring great satisfaction to all concerned.

A major task for both the adoptive parents and adopted child is to feel that the newcomer is an intrinsic part of the family. This is why I think it is a mistake to tell a child from birth it was adopted, or to maintain so-called "open adoptions" where the biological parent

(s) are involved in the life of the adopted child, or to immerse children adopted from foreign cultures in enrichment programs acquainting them with the culture of their origin. While well intended, I think these agendas are all misguided. There are professionals, however, who think otherwise. I think all of the above complicate an adoptee's task of feeling fully integrated and a part of the adoptive family. This achievement is necessary for later individuation to take place and its absence has major implications for the developing personality of the child, which will be discussed in Chapter 7.

I advise not telling the child until it is older, if this is possible. Often it is impossible because friends, relatives and acquaintances talk openly about the child's adoption. Adoption across racial lines also makes this impossible. Ideally, my minimum age would be eight. At eight years of age, for most youngsters, there occurs a major maturational cognitive change, a shift from sensory-motor to concrete operations. This is a change from simple perceptual and motor responses to the world to a more rational, organized and conceptual way of engaging things and people in the surrounding world. A child's ability to comprehend a parent's personal narrative will be easier at this older age.

I wish to distinguish my advocacy of delaying disclosure of the fact of adoption from what is called a family secret. With the latter there is no intent to tell the facts ever to the child, whereas I am guided by the intention of delaying the telling until a more propitious time. A family secret is in the context of shame, whereas my rationale is the capacity to understand and maintenance of a sense of "family-belonging."

Most adoptive parents elect to tell adoptees they were adopted from "day one." The explanation is in the context of how much they were "wanted" by the adoptive parents. If the child is of a different race from the adoptive parents then withholding the knowledge of adoption cannot be accomplished. If this is so, a parent can help a child by being truthful about the facts when the child becomes curious about their biological parents. This can be difficult for some adoptive parents who feel they are the "true" parents of the child and they may feel discarded and competitive with the biological parents. But such curiosity is natural, especially for an adolescent or young adult contemplating becoming a parent him or herself. There are agencies that can be of help to an adoptee with such a quest. Biological parents differ as to whether or not they welcome contact with the child given up for adoption. For many it reawakens all the old feelings long since buried that were felt at the time of giving up their baby for adoption. Some reunions are successful, while others are not. When they are successful adoptees will feel enriched by having new people in their lives. In instances where it is unsuccessful a new felt rejection must be dealt with. Sometimes the adoptee discovers a full or half biological sib that was not given up for adoption. This is particularly hard to reconcile with one's own personal history. The "family romance" fantasy, discussed fully in the chapter below dealing with the Oedipal Complex, is an additional potentially complicating and confusing factor for adoptive children, and another consideration of mine for opposing open adoptions.

More and more partners of the same gender are either adopting or, in the case of a lesbian couple one partner seeks artificial insemination. Again, we have insufficient experience with such couples or their children to offer much advice to these parents and their children. The obvious question is "What are the effects upon a child to have both parents be the same gender?" What if you are a boy and have two mothers or a girl having two fathers? We have an *a priori* hunch that it will be confusing. I think that such a couple, usually well educated and informed according to existing demographic data, go to lengths to expose their children to adults of each gender. In this manner, children can learn about the various gender roles in our society and have opportunities to identify with an adult of the same gender as their own. Presumably, the parents help their children process questions and concerns about being different from peers. In recent generations, divergences in life style and ethnic and racial origins are not infrequent so children from these backgrounds are now considered less exotic.

Chapter 4

The Toddler Years/Anal [Urethral] Phase

The toddler period roughly begins when a child starts to be able to walk, albeit uncertainly to begin with. Children differ as to when this happens but usually by twelve months of age a child will start to get around, toddle, in an upright position without holding onto to things like furniture. Earlier children are able to crawl or scoot around but the advent of upright locomotion introduces a "new world" to them. Secure in the foundation of an attachment to their parent, they feel more comfortable to venture forth into this new world, leaving the fond embrace of mother or father.

Look upon the face of a toddler who is toddling about and you see exuberance and joy. For a parent to see a toddler standing upright and moving about without holding on is equally a joyous occasion. But it is also a sad one for **both** parties. For the parent, her or his little baby is growing up. There is a feeling of loss connected with another sign of separateness. For the toddler the joyful expression can disappear after a fall or when he or she realizes that mother or father is not standing alongside. Toddlers may need to return to the side of parents to touch them, sight not being reassuring enough. This simple fact is also very profound. All of us from early on must come to terms with acceptance that each new acquired skill results in a mini-loss insofar as a parent will no longer be there to do the task for you or with you. Every child needs a mother to leave and in the process establishes a sense of his or her own individuality or identity. For some this accumulative feeling of loss proves too much and they reassert their dependency and take on a characteristic immaturity. Separation becomes a major issue for these children. It is helpful to young children to alert them when you are leaving the room and reassure them you will be returning very shortly. "Fred, mommy is going to the bathroom and will be back very soon."

Parents, predominantly mothers who are usually more involved with daily care, intuitively know this, so they allow for the autonomy to occur gradually. For awhile they will do things for toddlers, after awhile they allow toddlers to try to accomplish tasks for themselves while they are close by smiling approvingly and supportively, and then they allow toddlers to do tasks independently. Toddlers notice the gleam in their parents' eyes as they increasingly act autonomously. This progression allows for the toddler to feel reassured and to develop a beginning sense of competence.

But toddlers are still very helpless in many ways and naturally need an adult to care for them. The human animal differs from many other animals that must have more inborn readiness skills and faster maturation in order to survive predators. The human animal will go through a long apprenticeship before he or she can adequately independently take care of him or herself. Parenting is a long-term job. This long-term dependence of the human child on its caregiver is coupled with a likely perception of her as omnipotent. The young child does not want to relinquish this omnipotence that he can imagine he shares by virtue of not being completely separate from the caregiver (mother). Hence, the ambivalence about becoming autonomous.

The toddler will begin to give verbal signs of self-awareness and a sense of identity. For example, they may refer to themselves by name, "Johnny want," and soon they will refer to themselves as "I." Sentences of a rudimentary kind are spoken, expressing demands. Parents will try to be very alert to decipher their child's early words. The readiness to use language is inborn and children acquire the dialect of their caregivers. Sometime during the toddler period children seem to recognize themselves in a mirror.

What is conveyed during the toddler period and following months is that toddlers are very willful. Setting limits is an essential parental assignment during these months. Issues of safety guide most parents. A child may not be able to do something autonomously but will insist on doing it. If attempting some motor act, like going down a step, can be accomplished safely, most parents will tolerate it, allowing their child to experience the pleasure and honing of a skill. Parent need to recognize shaming is not the way to control their child. Taking the time to explain in terms that the youngster can understand is important. Remember, even at this young age children understand more than they can verbally communicate. They are guided by a resolute tone to understand their parent opposes an action.

Parents do well to treat their toddler respectfully. Even though the toddler has not much language they are beginning to understand the emotional intent behind words. Manners are taught by example. Parents who talk to their children politely are more likely to have well-mannered older children who will have the social awareness to treat all people civilly and with courtesy.

Some children are more active than others. Temperament seems to be inborn. If parents are basically passive and placid and their child is similar, this is a more compatible arrangement than if the child seems to be active and persistent. In the latter instance, parents will need to accommodate to their child's temperament. This is more realistic than to expect it to be the other way around. Some parents find this difficult. Some children are easy to please and the day with them seems seamless going from one activity to another. With other children, transitions are not easy, they are hard to satisfy and do not easily accept a substitute gratification if the one they seek is unavailable. Such children are challenging to even an experienced mother, so a mother best be forgiving of herself if she is finding such a child to be a challenge. It is helpful to young children to give them a "heads-up" that a transition will soon be taking place. "Sarah, very soon you will have to stop playing and get dressed to go to "play group."

The so-called "anal phase" of development will likely begin and overlap with oral urges by the age of two, more reliably by two and one half, and can be prominent until the child is nearly four years old. This phase of drive development is inborn, like its predecessor, and also has an urgent quality for expression. It is this that fuels the willfulness of the older toddler (two year old). Whereas earlier, the mouth, or oral cavity, seemed to be the child's focus of activity, now the anus becomes the focus. The time of toilet mastery is upon us. We prefer toilet "mastery" to "training" because the aim is to help a child develop a sense of mastery over bodily urges, not to feel like an automaton responding to a stimulus. The sense of mastery over bodily urges is important and begun at this early age will be consolidated in adolescence. That is, it takes a long period of time before a child feels more confident that they have some semblance of control over desires or urges that are originally physiological but take on a psychological coloring, too, e.g., hunger, sexual needs, etc.

The first stage of the anal phase includes a quality of expulsive elimination to the psychophysiological urge to defecate. The young child is deriving pleasure from expelling its feces with great destructive force. In the second stage a toddler will obtain pleasure by exercising withholding and control over its bowel movements. Later on in the process of toilet mastery the child becomes aware that elimination of body products seem to provide pleasure not only to him or herself but also to the parent. Most parents make a "big deal" when the child eliminates. They smile and praise the toddler. The elimination of stools takes on the quality of a gift from the child to the parent. But it is confusing to the child insofar as the gift is flushed away and disappears. Older children may become defiant and are ambivalently cooperative in complying with the parent's requests they deposit their gift in the toilet and not in their diaper. This ambivalence spreads to the way they treat their parents, showing affection and hurting them in close succession. The child responds to its stools in a concretized fashion. I mean by this that the stools are treated like family members. The biggest are said to be the daddy, with the smallest being the child, with the mommy in between.

The pleasure the child takes in withholding and then finally eliminating its stools has an erogenous or sexual quality. We know this from the analyses of adults and from self-reports from adults honest enough to remark about the pleasurable feeling of a well-formed bowel movement. The inborn erogeneity of the buttocks and anus is topic that we all are socialized to be very private about, unlike the erogeneity of the oral zone which is more acceptable and is permitted to be publicly acknowledged, such as via kissing, or even implied in eating something succulent, or drinking something sweet and warm.

The pleasure derived from anality is not only erogenous; it is also derived from aggressive urges. The admixture of the two drive expressions is called "sadism." Sadism evolves into pleasure obtained from controlling another person or from causing others pain. The pleasure in controlling another person originates in the pleasure in controlling one's stools. Temporarily, children may be sadistic towards insects or pets. Most children are socialized not to be sadistic.

It is **essential** at this point to make a distinction between "wishing" and "wanting." **Another way to put it is to distinguish "thoughts" from "deeds." Psychoanalysts do not equate the two.** As stated earlier, there is a world of difference between having a sadistic wish (thought or fantasy) and enacting the wish. So to say all children are capable of a sadistic thoughts is not to say that all children are sadists. But we do know, unfortunately, that the human species is capable of such behavior. An example would be the atrocities committed by the Nazis against humanity. When sadism turns against the self we call it "masochism," a pleasure derived from suffering (psychologically or physically) or surrendering to another's will. Fantasies of a child being beaten may be present in derivative form in latency age children. Fantasies involving coercion and submission regarding sex wherein one is perpetrator and/or recipient (sado-masochism) may be present in adults. Recall my earlier comments about active and passive aims in instinctual expression.

It is difficult for most adults to accept that children can have base instincts like sexual and destructive ones. We prefer to think of children as 'pure" and innocent. We must recognize that the human species is part of the animal kingdom. We are now civilized but our basic animal needs still exist in us, albeit for the most part not in the conscious part of our minds. Children must be taught to be civilized. As "domesticated" animals of the highest degree (we prefer "civilized") we usually are far removed from the jungle and hold ourselves to humanistic ideals. The uncivilized urges residing in the unconscious part of our mind may come out in our dreams and fantasies, and in transformed ways via the creative arts, but usually not in actions. Recent research suggests that in the latter half of the first year, babies prefer to look at or reach for things that help rather than have hindered.

Does this suggest an inherent morality? Perhaps, a biological inherent trend having to do with survival that culture needs to reinforce.

Let us return to our toddler. In general, toilet mastery should not be rushed. Patience and support of the child is very much called for. Children will differ as to how cooperative they will be in the process. It seems to have some connection to how innately strong the anal drive is. If it is not very strong then they will not be so insistent that they be in command of when and how they gratify its expression. If it is a strong urge they will struggle to express it and defy the parent's cajoling them to be "clean." It is with the latter child that a parent needs to avoid a control battle. Such a child will come around and comply at his or her own pace, albeit with some children not till around the ages of four to five. The rewards of becoming clean and identification with older peers and friends will eventually result in toilet mastery for almost all children. It is the rare child who is encopretic, a syndrome where a child soils indiscriminately as to time and place. I will have more to say about establishing toilet mastery in Chapter 8.

Parents during the earlier oral phase were faced with the same issue about having a child transform the manner of gratification with regard to weaning either from the breast or bottle. Some children compared to others have a strong urge to suck while other could care less. For parents, their own history of nursing (sucking) and toilet mastery will be unconscious determinants in how easy or difficult it will be for them to traverse their child's seeking of pleasure of these early in-born drives. I could state this for each developmental phase that your child passes through. Parents who are aware of their own "hot spots" or "buttons" may avoid making inappropriate demands or providing inappropriate indulgences that their child either cannot meet nor is seeking regarding the expression and eventual regulation of early childhood drives. A parent might "insist" that a less than two year old child use the toilet (deprivation.) Or a parent might delay encouraging their child to use a "potty" even though they are overtly displaying curiosity (indulgence). Such inappropriate demands or indulgences (either too much deprivation or gratification) lead to vulnerabilities in their child around which later neurotic conflicts can form. We call these vulnerabilities fixations. There seems to be an inverse relation-ship between the strength of an inborn component instinct and the quantity of deprivation or indulgence to result in a fixation (comple-mental series). Later in Chapters 5 & 8, the nature of neurotic conflicts will be discussed.

Towards the end of the anal phase, interest in urination comes to the fore, so a focus on the anus is shared with the urethra. This marks a phase called the "urethral phase." Boys take pleasure in their urinary stream. Did you ever see a boy around four or five or even older given the task of using a hose to water the garden? Often there is sheer de-light. Remnants of this pleasure can be seen in the derivative pleasure some boys later take in spitting. Girls like to look at their urinary stream too and are sometimes envious that boys can stand and urinate and that a boy's urinary stream is more forceful than their own.

Adults often inappropriately tickle children and the outcome of-ten is a need to urinate on the child's part. Children when excited will often urinate presumably because the excitement has become sexual in quality. Because of immaturity of their genital systems, urination occurs, and not ejaculation for boys, and not vaginal lubrication for girls.

As mentioned earlier, during the later toddler months, there is a growth spurt in speech and language sophistication. This acquisition of an inborn readiness will result in more effective communication between parent and child. Parents from then on will continually be telling their child to "use your words."

The more this is successful the more likely frustrations will not mount for both children and parents. This is a gradual process and parents must be patient. As a child gets older the ability increases to employ mental processes ("defenses") that will help in reducing the intensity and imperiousness of needs. With greater mental maturity more complex thinking processes become available. If a child can daydream gratification, thereby deriving partial gratification, a substi-tute for an unavailable desired source of gratification might be more acceptable to the child. The use of action as a means of communication is readily available to children and will be so through adolescence. It is only gradually that symbolic thought and words can replace action as a preferred mode of communication. Internal thought is a form of trial action insofar as different outcomes can be considered and one chosen that is expected to end with a desired outcome that is adaptive and in the best interest of the child or adolescent. For some children action feels more real or authentic because it is irrevocable while thought is silent and changeable.

The more children can use words to discharge feelings, the less reliance on somatic, bodily channels of expression. Bodily means of expression of feelings might be via aches and pains, perspiration, diarrhea, hyperactivity, etc. Preferred means of bodily expression of tension is noticeable very early in a child's life and will be retained for most of a person's life. Some adults when stressed are more likely to get headaches, others to get diarrhea, still others to sweat, and so on. Differentiating somatic feelings, e.g., hunger or pain, from emotional feelings, e.g., sadness or anxiety, is a gradual process not achieved in a reliable way till the early Latency years. We will speak more about the various mental maneuvers that the mind employs when we consider the Latency phase of development in Chapter 9.

Children love to run around nude during their early years. Perhaps you remember the exhilaration yourself when you were a late toddler or early preschooler? Adults are often uneasy about allowing this. Perhaps, there is a worry about easy access to masturbation or to elimination in the wrong places? Nakedness is a natural inclination for the child. Exhibitionistic pleasure and delight in unrestrained motility seem to be involved. Alas, children do need to be socialized and to learn that modesty is the norm of civil society and this childhood pleasure will need to be given up. They can learn this without being shamed and will accommodate themselves to this expectation of society. Displaying one's body and looking at another's seems to be inborn desires that bring pleasure for all people. With time such desires evolve into concern about attractiveness, adornment and physical fitness. Regretfully, our culture has capitalized upon this and has commercialized vanity to the point that some teenagers and adults are preoccupied with how they look to others. With a minority, dieting can become a pathological enterprise. I will say more about this when I consider the stages of adolescence.

Children at this age do not easily share toys with other children. Also they may grab something being held by another toddler. At this young age they are self-centered and it will take some learning before they can share and tolerate the frustration of "taking turns." They engage in "parallel play," whereby the activity they are engaged in can be the same one that another toddler is busy with but there does not occur interaction between the two toddlers. This, too, will change during the latter pre-school years.

Chapter 5
The Preschool Years/ Phallic Phase

Preschool requires the child to deal for a period of time with a teacher, an adult different from his or her parents. Up till entry into preschool most other adults dealt with in the absence of parents likely have been relatives. A baby sitter may be an exception but this encounter usually is within the familiarity of the child's home. I advise that mothers or fathers be present when a 2 year old has a preschool experience and that it be only for a few hours a couple of times a week. I hold this as an ideal, maybe unrealistic in most families and I will discuss day care in the next chapter. The majority of two year olds are not ready to spend a lot of time away from their mothers. Children must have the capacity to evoke and sustain an internal image in their mind of the mother or other significant caregiver. The image needs to be sustained even when they have a physical or psychological need in their parent's absence, or when the need is fulfilled. When such needs exist and a parent is absent the evocation of anxiety followed by rage or apathy is likely. The stability of the mental image of the parent must be able to withstand the rage and not be obliterated. If it is unable to be sustained, intense anxiety will follow. This capacity usually occurs reliably around 36 months. We call this capacity the establishment of object constancy. Essentially the process involves being able to feel the presence of a real person in the external world to now "inhabit" the inner world. A prominent psychoanalyst has termed this a "presence in an absence."

It is not that unusual in a preschool setting to see a youngster carrying a valued blanket or soft animal. You know from our earlier discussion that we call such things transitional objects. You will recall we call them such because the child is transitioning from self-investment to self-other differentiation. We conjecture that transitional objects are experienced as both as an aspect of the self and of the part object (in most instances the mother). We conjecture that the child is feeling the loss or absence of the soothing maternal figure and uses the transitional object to try to conjure up the experience of her presence, e.g., the mother's scent, in her absence. Usually, such transitional objects wither away in importance, as the child gets older. Some parents, however, prefer that their distressed child seek them out for comfort. Parents are advised to let this process occur naturally and not to expedite it by throwing away the transitional object. This can be vey upsetting to a youngster. In some instances an older child or even an adult can lapse into a reverie type mood when listening to music or smelling a particular scent, etc. Such phenomena create a transitional mood. We conjecture that at such moments an individual is feeling a primordial emotional connection to an early self-other experience for which there is no words.

A sophisticated nursery school will accommodate itself to the dependency needs of the children and will introduce a graduated separation period of parent and child. What this means is that parents may be in the same classroom with the child for a period of time, perhaps days, then in the building so that if their child becomes inconsolable they can be available. Once the child is comfortable transitioning to the teacher the parent should exit quickly. Parents need to accept at pickups that their child may ignore them for some minutes or become dramatically whiney as a punishment for "abandoning" them. I advise parents to try not to take it personally and soon such dramatizations will stop. Additionally, parents are encouraged to keep in touch with teachers so after the school day they can talk with their child about their experiences. Children react to the emotional moods of peers, so that if a child in their class is grieving the loss of a pet, it is helpful that parents are aware of this classroom news to make more sense of their children and to be helpful to them in processing the news. Towards the end of entry in preschool, a parent may start to feel uneasy about the transition to kindergarten, especially if it is a full day one. One's child is growing up and a parent will be dealing with the end of an era. Soon the child will be going out into the bigger community. Although more self reliant, the child is still very dependent upon his parent. Some children, too, start to anticipate the longer day away from mother, but they are usually eager for the move to "big school." These feelings will be revisited for both child and parent in the transition period from high school to college.

The three year old is usually dealing with the beginning of the so-called "phallic phase" of drive development, overlapping with the earlier onset anal and urethral phases. Remnants of the earliest oral phase will coexist, too. The phallic phase will last usually up until five or six years of age. The term "phallic phase" has been justifiably criticized because of its male focus but another label has not been commonly accepted. "Phallic" originally was proposed because it was believed that both boys and girls seemed to think of themselves as boys during the early part of this phase. This notion has been modified in contemporary psychoanalytic thinking. We now believe that girls value and are interested in their own genitals and the interior space that they have and boys do not. During the phallic phase, for both boys and girls, the genitals are a focus of pleasure. Masturbatory behavior begins and parents often admonish their children, "Don't touch yourself." The boy values his penis and becomes anxious that an injury to it could occur or he could have it taken from his body ("castration anxiety"). Some girls may believe they, too, once had a penis. Boys notice girls do not have a penis and in their egocentricity assume girls once had one like them which confirms their belief their own penis is in peril. Actually the term "castration" is a misnomer insofar as it refers to the testicles.

Boys behave like penetrating missiles, often hurling their bodies through space. Girls begin to play with dolls in maternal ways. Boys will build towers out of blocks and girls' build harbors suggestive of an inner space (the uterus?). At this early stage of the phallic phase, both genders are beginning to become aware of gender differences. They will notice that females have breasts and men do not, that males have facial hair and females do not, etc. In a few months, the phallic feelings will be elaborated to take into account gender differences and discriminative responses are manifested. This occurs with progressive entry into what is called the "Oedipal Phase," to be discussed in Chapter 7.

"Penis envy," a concept that describes and conceptualizes about feelings in young girls, once was believed to be ubiquitous in girls. It was conceptualized that girls wished that they had a penis and treated their clitoris as if it was a diminutive penis. We used to think that girls as they got older adopted total body narcissism as a compensation for the penis they lack. This could be achieved by later interest in fashion, body shapeliness, and via adornment, e.g., use of makeup and jewelry. As indicated above, we now appreciate much more that girls are interested in their vulva as the entrance to a valued interior space in which a baby might grow. Mothers should use the scientific names for female genitalia and distinguish the different anatomical parts. This will help demystify the girl's genitals that are harder to see than a boy's and subject to a greater sense of the "unknown." Boys, on the other hand, have always envied girls' abilities to have babies.

People ubiquitously envy what the other has and they do not possess. I believe as our culture has become less male-privileged, women have more pride in their gender and more self-respect. Mothers have modeled greater acceptance of their femininity, so that their daughters are more pleased with their genital differences, and penis envy is observed less and less. Women now have more opportunities than before regarding career choice and they are confidently and competently engaging in them. In previous generations, they may have agreed that many careers were privileges of men. For many women, however, careers outside the home have not been an issue. For these women, being a full time homemaker and caregiver is fulfilling.

The women's liberation movement has raised the consciousness of many women who were dissatisfied as to their intrinsic self-worth. Contemporary young fathers have become more involved in hands-on childcare than previous generations. Perhaps, this is a side effect of changes in women that has allowed men to re-examine masculinity and resulted in an adaptive way for men to deal with envy of procreation.

Infants seem to appreciate the mock affect of their parents, who, e.g., exaggerate surprise very early on to the delight of their infant. It appears to an observer that the infant understands it to be a pretense.

If you watch mothers with infants when they are calming their child you may notice them telling the child a story about themselves as a child being distressed and then calmed. The infant may even be pre-verbal but an observer gets a sense of comprehension on the infant's part. The infant begins to be calmed. As the child gets older he may use a story similar to one he has been told countless times with dolls and toy animals. This copying of mother's narrative may be the beginning of pretend play. While pretending in play seems to be available in the second year it stabilizes the following year for a child.

Up until three years of age, young children have had contacts with other children of limited durations, but now as a preschooler they have moved from parallel play to cooperative fantasy play with peers. During parallel play, we have noted how two young children playing alongside one another, perhaps with blocks, seem to ignore one another. Children in fantasy play can pretend and assign roles to each other and a plot is enacted. "You're the Daddy and I'm the mommy and you can be the baby." Peer relationships have to be dealt with. Dominance and submissiveness need to be negotiated and accommodated. Fantasy play will allow the child to pretend to be adults they experience in their life, e.g., the mailmen, policeman, teacher, nurse, doctor, father, mother, etc. Enactment of these roles helps children to sort out the multiplicity of relationships that they observe adult people to be engaged in. Also themes having to do with complicated issues like competition, monsters, heroes, etc., will be dramatized in fantasy play. Themes will deal with who is the "strongest" parent, who is the scariest "ghost," and whether "Superman" or "Spiderman" is the best hero. Incomprehensible notions to immature minds, such as "death," are enacted in play with peers and while still a mystery may become less scary. Toys and costumes increasingly are used as props and facilitators of the narrative.

Play helps children become aware of feelings and to label them, thereby allowing them to be more accessible and open to regulation by the child. Play originates as the child nurses and touches the breast or puts its finger into its mother's mouth. Perhaps the first toy is mother's nipple or a child's own fingers. As it evolves, play is a way children bring into conscious awareness scary feelings and accompanying thoughts in a venue that is different from the original scary one. Children customarily avoid being self-reflective about frightening experience or imaginings. In play what was scary or traumatic may not be altered but the stage on which it is re-experienced is different so that there can be abreaction (discharge of feeling) and integration of the experience in a manageable way. Many a young child after a visit to the doctor or dentist has pretended to be the professional examining a patient (another child or a doll). Hence, via playing and pretending children can turn a scary experience passively endured into an active re-creation in which they do the scaring. Such play helps them to become less fearful of imagined scary figures and less stricken by real ones.

Are there some toys that should be avoided? What I particularly have in mind is whether or not to select toys that are representative of weapons, usually given to boys, and Barbie dolls, usually given to girls. While I do not see the sense of giving toy weapons resembling real ones to children based on my value system that values the preservation of life rather than its destruction, I believe it is a misguided belief that violent play by a child encourages violence in later life. In most instances, children and not adults will select what they play out, and if they so choose they can pretend anything, e.g., a block, to be a gun or knife in an enacted scenario. They may be attempting in a pretend way to master something violent that they witnessed or heard about. But I caution you about concluding this is so insofar as they may be dealing instead with age appropriate internal issues that are temporary and get sorted out via such play. If violent enactments, however, were the only theme whenever they engaged in pretend play, then, I would be alerted to the possibility that something might be amiss for the child and I would try to engage him or her in conversation about their interest in such scenarios. If something is bothering a child a teacher's or parent's attentiveness and clarification may be supportive and may be even sufficient to help a child to resolve what is preoccupying.

For very young girls, an important consideration for me as to whether or not to provide your daughter a Barbie doll is that it is a representation of an adult, not a baby. A little girl wants to cuddle and mother a doll that looks more like her, not one that looks more like her mother. Hence, a soft doll would be welcomed. Often she uses the Barbie doll to represent an older girl or a mother. Barbie dolls have recently received a lot of media attention because it was the fiftieth anniversary of their introduction onto the market. Many people object to them because the doll portrays an image of women that conveys that conventional beauty is the ideal for girls to aspire to. Its popularity with girls is thought by some to underlay the self-consciousness of girls about their bodies' appearance. My own belief is that Barbie dolls do not cause this but are more a reflection of our culture's idealization of this image of women. I think that an array of different dolls can be provided to introduce divergences in body shape, appearance, and clothes styles to help girls to value themselves more. Also, mothers can be very helpful to their daughters in modeling acceptance of one's own body type and taste in clothes.

Many preschools include the topic of the life cycle in their curriculum. A child will learn that although leaves die the tree does not. They will learn that in the spring, new leaves grow from the buds on the trees. They will plant seeds and watch sprouts grow and then flowers appear and bloom. Then the flowers will wither and die. There may be an aquarium with fish. Baby fish will be born and some fish will die. Perhaps there will be hamsters or gerbils and also births and deaths. It is via these observations that children will be introduced to the topics of death and regeneration, making the former a little less mysterious and scary. Most importantly, there will be an adult who will be listening to a child's questions and helping to process the answers.

During these years a pet may be introduced into the family. Sometimes, parents wait until a child is old enough to be responsible for some of the care of the pet. This will not be until late latency years in most cases. In some families prior to having children, a couple will have a pet so when a baby joins the family a pet already is a member. A pet can be a very important companion for a child. The young child may be a little rough in showing affection towards the pet and an adult may need to be aware of this possibility and instruct the child. Other children may be too controlling of the pet. Children will use their pet dog or cat to express feelings that they are uncomfortable expressing towards others. Parents will need to be aware of this and educate their child about how the pet also has feelings. This is a good opportunity for helping children to regulate the expression of feelings. Parents need to be aware when getting a puppy that is not housebroken if their child is gaining toilet mastery simultaneously. The methods of toilet mastery will be different and confusing to the child. Adults can be harsh with their puppies. You certainly do not want to put the puppy's nose close to the mess it has made and say "bad Rufus!" within a young child's sight or hearing. Remember, too, a puppy has feelings.

Issues of self- esteem and a beginning sense of morality that began to be inculcated in the home are reinforced in the preschool setting. Sharing and taking turns and cleaning up your own mess are tasks that the teacher is helping the kids in her charge to consider and struggle with. The good teacher works to strengthen the parental bond and not to usurp it with regard to rules and expectations. The child will lapse often in efforts to be fair, generous, and truthful, because the "inner helper," i.e. the conscience, is not yet consolidated. The experienced teacher knows this and does not shame, humiliate or threaten the transgressing child. She, like a savvy parent, will help the child process events such as when Bobby grabbed Johnny's toy and the latter hit the former in retaliation. She is helping Johnny use his words to confront Bobby with the unfairness of his action and restrain from hitting him and thereby demonstrating what colleagues have felicitously labeled "emotional muscle." Self-expression within the confines of self-regulation is reinforced.

Helping children to process events, as mentioned earlier, beneficially begins in infancy. It is a multi-year process for the child to go from expressing feelings via the body, to fantasy, and then via secondary, higher-order symbolic mental functioning to abstract thinking. We now believe that children first have implicit knowledge about their bodily experiences. Essentially this is a non-verbal form of knowing. As children get older, explicit knowing augments experiencing. Memories based upon implicit knowing will be somatic and non-verbal (procedural memory). You may revisit a specific early childhood locale and become tense, start to sweat, and not know why because you banished the frightful image from your conscious mind. This is likely because you experienced something scary or painful before you even had words to label it. Some of these memories will involve early experiences of self-other (part-object) before language was used. Once you acquire words, memories, explicit memory, will include the words. "I remember being very young and being scared by a big dog here." The attaching of words, too, makes the memory more accessible to consciousness. Memories are organized into systems of procedural and explicit memories. This system is called the "mnemic" or "memorial system."

Separation and unavailability of the mother for the baby (deprivation) as well as mother's presence and responsiveness to the infant's needs (satisfaction) both promote memories. Eventually, a stable mental image of mother (object constancy) capable of being revived in her absence and during experiences of need and in the absence of need will be established. Repeated such experiences are involved in helping the child eventually to distinguish perceptions from memories, and outer from inner.

The establishment of a system of memories is an essential part of the mind. Subjectively, it might even feel as if they are one and the same thing. Memories allow for continuity and meaning to our lives. The past is compared to the present and the future is imagined in connection with the here-and-now. Sometimes memories can screen earlier or later memories. Remembering is not a simple matter, being influenced by feelings (e.g., recalling pleasurable events, usually more so, than un-pleasurable ones). Very frightening memories, traumatic in quality, are best affirmed as historical reality when sufficient conviction exists that this is so. There might be a tendency to insist on them being a subjective distortion of objective events. In some instances this could be so. Distinguishing the two can often be an important part of treatment. Traumatic memories are sort of frozen in time, often dissociated from feeling.

Helping children to think about their thoughts is invaluable in helping children to appreciate (likely sometime at the end of the second year) that they have a mind, and that others do, too, and that their mind and its contents can be different from others. "You see me smiling but you are not." This leads to what has been called the process of mentalization, a kind of self-reflectiveness or theory of mind. It helps children in the process of becoming separate individuals, i.e., to keep separate the internal representation of themselves from that of others. This facilitates empathy and relationships with other people. Awareness of others also having a similar capacity facilitates cooperative fantasy play. It also aids in the development of higher order mental functioning, e.g., fantasying or pretending. Another way to put it would be to say a child begins to appreciate psychic reality. If you know you have a mind, you can imagine events outside of your mind within your mind. "Mommy is in the car returning from shopping and she'll be here soon." Parents help their children engage in this process throughout childhood.

This cognitive development also heralds recognition for the child that they are capable of "private" thoughts that others are not privy to. Presumably, this encourages fantasying. It will take at least a couple of more years, maybe longer, before a child will abandon the idea that a parent(s) can read his or her mind. Parents, too, accept that their child is entitled to have private thoughts. For children to value the *privacy* of their mind and for parents to accept this, is linked to an emotional acceptance by both parties of the separateness of each from the other. With increasing age, the voluntary sharing of private thoughts with another person leads to intimacy. For some children and later as adults, having secrets is understood to be like having power and control over people with whom silence is used like a weapon. Establishing intimacy for some people is fraught with anxiety.

The ability to fantasize, in turn, is a way station to more symbolic and abstract thinking. Later on, when the child confidently knows the difference between real and pretend, fantasying particularly is an asset. During this mental activity, reality can be deliberately suspended. In a fantasy, a person can partially gratify any wish that is deprived in reality. A child can imagine riding a bicycle that he wished for but did not get as a birthday present. Frustration tolerance is not pushed to its limits. When children are excessively frustrated, the tension experienced from the deprivation tips self-regulation and major emotive disruption of functioning occurs. Often less mature functioning occurs along with anger.

The earliest fantasies, primal fantasies that likely are never accessible to the conscious mind, we speculate to involve bodily experiences having to do with physical closeness to mother who becomes the infant's object of desire. Once the infant singles out mother as the most important object, separation from her causes distress. We speculate that the infant, under the sway of oral impulses, orally incorporates the mother. This creates an unconscious feeling of union with mother.

Earlier, in Chapter 2, I talked about "psychic reality" and contrasted it to "objective reality." If this is not enough for people of all ages, especially children, to learn to distinguish, contemporary children (adults too) need to come to comprehend "virtual reality." This is computer generated simulated reality. Sometimes stereoscopic glasses add a three dimensional quality. How confusing it must be for a young mind to talk on the telephone with a family member. Where is the person the toddler or preschooler must be wondering? Now, imagine telecommunication on Skype, and add to the confusion.

It is important for young children to acquire a sense of predictability about their environment. If they have such, they will feel safe. Feeling safe is a basic need and connected to this feeling is the consolidation of the reality principle. An important aspect of this principle is knowing the difference between a perception and a thought, or as mentioned above, the difference between psychic and objective reality.

Characteristic of thinking during the early years is animistic thinking, a belief in magic. Thinking having a magical quality causes a belief that a wish or thought actually will occur. This is because of the child's irrational belief in the power of thoughts (omnipotence). This kind of thinking temporarily helps a child to deal with a feeling of relative helplessness. But if it persists, it can lead to serious difficulties. It is irrational to believe that thoughts directly cause actions. Belief otherwise will reduce initiative and being proactive. More so, an older child could feel responsible, for example, if in a fit of anger they wish a sibling to get hit by a car and this coincidentally happens. Serious guilt will follow.

Many parents inadvertently reinforce magical thinking in their well intentioned but misguided wish to keep alive the excitement of early childhood by the promulgation of certain myths. I'm thinking of myths such as "Santa Claus," and assorted portrayals of the supernatural. But it is present in numerous explanations of reality based on non-scientific, irrational thinking.

You might be thinking, "Come on, you're such a spoil sport. What harm can it do if a child gets some fun out of enchantment or a belief in miracles?" Fairy tales are forms of enchantment but they are presented to a child in the context of a conscious decision to allow for the suspension of reality to enjoy a story of pretend. I think you can contextualize explanations within the frame of imagination and pretend and still have fun. If they are not they should be, in my judgment, and questions for clarification that are asked by young listeners should be answered truthfully (factually). "Daddy, are fairies real?" "No son, we have fun pretending that fairies are real." I believe the same principle holds for stories about mythical characters like Santa Claus. When young children are told that heaven is a real place "up in the sky," they take it quite literally, along with portrayals of angels. If, additionally, a young child is told that stars embody people who have "died" but are not "really" dead and the twinkling is a proof of this, a young child's belief is reinforced about the impermanency of death.

Due to the tenuous hold on what is "real" and what is "pretend" for the young child, picture books with animals as characters that talk may cause confusion to a young child. Parents may have little choice insofar as most children's picture books are illustrated with animals. It makes more sense to me to illustrate the stories with pictures of people if its reality that you are trying to reinforce for young children. As they get older and the distinction is clear between the real world and "make believe world," imaginary characters will be fun.

Sometimes young children create imaginary companions whom they talk to and have seated next to themselves. Intelligent children are more likely to create such a companion. This does not mean that if your child has no imaginary companion that he or she is unintelligent. A child will often use the imagined companion to attribute to them their own behaviors unapproved by parents or their own early conscience. It might be a thought and not an action that is attributed. "Jimmy (the imagined companion) told me he wants to pull Becky's (sister) hair." The child will wait to see the parent's reaction. It is as if they are adaptively "testing the waters" via such a play. Parents can play along and not try to convince the child of the non-existence of the imagined companion. Doing so will only upset the child and serves no purpose. They might ask, "What did you tell Jimmy?" An imaginary companion gets less important as the child gets older.

Halloween is a difficult holiday for young children. It is becoming one of the major holidays in the States. The costumes and images are scary. Imagine taking a pre-school age child "trick-or-treating." You go up to a house with skeletons hanging from trees and jack-o-lanterns lit up on the porch. The door opens and a woman dressed as a witch opens the door. I'll wager that your young child will be frightened. Parents can try to bypass this occurrence by pre-arranging to only go to friends' homes, but probably have to pass houses decorated for Halloween to get there. I suggest having a party at home until the child gets older and understanding differences between pretend and real is consolidated.

Preschool is a time of learning through play but also helping children with cognitive skills. While cognitive skills should not be neglected, my bias is in favoring learning through play. I think that for the preschooler, play is a natural way for the intense feelings and bodily/mental urges to be expressed and controlled in a safe way. Also, ideas of conception, even if false, can be enacted. In a preschool environment cognitive skills are introduced such as learning to read and write. By the time children enter kindergarten, they have some rudimentary cognitive skills such as the ability to write their name, remember the alphabet, and read simple words. Preschoolers who are interested in reading will attempt to read signs they see from trips in the car or read words on the cereal box. Social skills are reinforced in interactions with peers and teachers.

I believe parents are beginning to teach "values" to their child from the very beginning of their life. If parents treat a child and others with respect, if parents are civil in dealing with others, if they are honest, if they persevere despite adversity, etc., then it is more likely that their child will adopt the same values. Parents serve as models, especially in their dealings with their child. Children eventually will internalize parental behavior and own it themselves and strive to realize these ideals. Other adults, e.g., relatives, teachers, coaches, religious leaders, etc., also serve as models.

For some parents dealing with teachers can be a problem. Insofar as their child, beginning in preschool, will have twelve or more years of schooling in which contact with teachers is likely, it is helpful to understand what might be the cause of the problem. For these parents feelings that arose when they were their child's age and they had to deal with teachers can be re-experienced. It is as if they are children dealing with adult teachers in the here-and-now. Understanding these unconscious repetitious phenomena from one's past, called "transference," might allow parents to get distance from their feelings and permit assuming a more adult role capable of advocating for their child, if necessary, vis-à-vis the teacher.

As a psychoanalyst I use the term "unconscious" a lot. This is because we contend that much of what motivates us is not in our conscious awareness. The mind is like an iceberg insofar as that which is conscious, i.e., in our metaphor, above water, is very little, while most of it is underwater. Despite being outside our awareness unconscious entities exert a motivational force on the mind. In some instances, bringing someone's attention to a thought or wish that they are unaware of may allow the person to become aware of it. In this case we speak of the thought or wish as preconscious. Primal images that were never conscious, in our theory preverbal, are unconscious. The majority of the constituents of the unconscious part of the mind are conceptualized as being thoughts (wishes, images, impulses, etc.) which were banished from consciousness and are blocked (repressed) and cannot re-enter consciousness except in a dream or the occasional daytime breakthrough of the repression barrier. Derivatives of unconscious impulses, images, ideas, thoughts, desires, and wishes, do enter our consciousness and it is these that we grapple with in every day life, in most instances in adaptive ways.

I now will introduce some more theory. I hope it will help you appreciate the complexity of a child's mind. The young child is still very much a creature of very strong drives and needs. In a psychoanalytic model of the mind, this is the part of the mind (Id) dominated by primordial inborn psychic needs that have biological bodily origins. These needs demand to be satisfied and the mind must deal with them. We call these needs by various names, e.g., instincts, urges, drives, wishes or desires. The two major drives are Eros (libido or sex) and aggression and their derivatives. Derivatives of these two major drives are numerous and account for much of motivation. Drives very early on seek external objects (people and/or things) in relation to which satisfaction is sought. The mind learns ways to control and regulate drives. Socialization, a process wherein children internalize societal values and learn skills, is one way to regulate intense inner drives and feelings. Societal values will dictate that the "raw" expression of a wish will be unacceptable. The wish will need to be modified or transformed to make it more acceptable. The child (really, the child's mind) may allow for a partial gratification in a day- or nocturnal dream.

In the psychoanalytic model of the mind we refer to the executive functions of the mind (Ego). These functions, (e.g., regulatory mental measures [defenses], perception, fantasying, judgment, reality testing, memory, etc.) comprise mainly the conscious part of the mind. The executive part of the mind "negotiates" with the inner and outer worlds. Our internalized moral code (both what is and is not allowed expression in action) and our standards (ideals) comprise another part of the mind (Superego).

The drives or desires are in conflict with the two major regulatory agencies of the mind, that comprising the executive functions and moral code. This conflict is what is meant when the term "mental dynamics" is used. Mental conflicts are **universal** and an on-going feature of life. I will say more about this later in Chapter 8. We help our children get a good start in this life-long struggle by helping them to think rationally and to be adaptive. Adaptation involves being cognizant of both inner and outer demands and arriving at sensible and creative solutions to conflicts. A major achievement of the mind is when intense feelings can be transformed into signal feelings, like a yellow light alerts an auto driver to an impending red light so they take steps to decelerate. There is a special feeling that alerts the mind to the pressure of an unconscious desire demanding active expression. We call this anxiety. The mind, upon which the demand is felt, anticipates danger in the form of punishment if the desire is expressed openly. Principal **imagined** dangers that seem to be universal are loss of the object [abandonment], loss of the object's love [e.g., mother's love], castration, and loss of the love of the conscience [experienced as the feeling of guilt]. You can see these imagined dangers all involve a loss. To avoid these punishments becomes a strong motivation to keep forbidden desires contained in some way. Anxiety as a signal alerts the mind to keep a forbidden wish (desire) from consciousness, or transform it, or to control it by not putting it into action. This is not a form of problem solving, but rather a dynamic mental process, aspects of which are unconscious. When the mind is unable to heed anxiety as a signal, panic is felt. This regulatory process takes years to consolidate in the form of a reliable internal "firewall". When the danger is conscious and not imagined but real we speak of fear.

We help our children to transform intense drive aims that are unacceptable to society into more acceptable ones. We call the process of transformation of the aims of sexual urges sublimation, e.g., changing a wish to mess with feces into a wish to sculpt clay. We call the transformation of aggressive wishes de-aggressivization, e.g., changing a wish to destroy living matter by pulling leaves off of a plant into a wish to nurture, by pruning. In the preschool venue, sublimation is given a head start in the encouragement of creativity and play, e.g., in finger painting in lieu of playing with one's own body products. Aggressiveness in preschool can be directed into competitiveness or into its opposite, cooperation.

Another way to understand regulation and transformation of instinctual wishes is to comprehend how the mind must learn greater tolerance of the instinctual demands made upon it. This does not mean, "giving into" the demand. This is where regulation and transformation come into play. Complete non-welcoming of unconscious wishes is not the ideal. A harmonious equilibrium involves communication between the unconscious and conscious parts of the mind. Recognition of an unconscious desire will not scare a mind that appreciates the significant difference between a wish and an act. Rather than "exiling" unconscious desire from conscious awareness, acknowledgment is acceptable. Integrating unconscious wishes might mean giving expression to some form of them in creative endeavors such as art, sport, play, drama, poetry, prose, etc., or in a dream. A psychoanalytically informed education recognizes the instinctual side of Man and attempts to benefit from its vitality while "taming" it.

As a child gets older the regulatory agencies of the mind mature. The initial consolidation of the regulatory parts of the mind, usually by six years of age, allows for increased utilization of higher order rational thinking and moral values. Mentation, or the mental processes of the mind, evolves from a primitive organization (primary process) to a higher organization (secondary process). Essentially, this higher organization comes about by the linking of words to images of things. It is with words that the mind becomes capable of reasoning. This in turn enables the child to process and control wishes.

It is essential for parents to realize that they will serve as auxiliaries to the immature mind of their child for a number of years. They will be his or her allies to help the child cope adaptively with inner (desires) and outer demands (rules, values). As an auxiliary ego, parents will help insure that a lack of preparedness on a child's part does not result in the child feeling overwhelmed and consequently traumatized. As an aspect of a parent serving as an auxiliary ego, a child feels valued and appreciated. Basic needs for children when satisfied help to build up healthy narcissism.

I hope this digression into a description of this model of the mind is helpful to you. You can appreciate how complicated the mind of a child is and how it will take years to consolidate the mind's "firewall" and how parents will need to be patient, clarifying, and supportive of their child's efforts to become rational, reasonable, and adaptable young men and women.

Chapter 6
Day Care

In the best of worlds, only one parent would need to work to be able to provide financially for the family. There would be a child allowance from the government to encourage one parent to refrain from employment outside the home, or employers would allow employees to split a full time job with a colleague and maintain benefits, and guaranteed job retention and career progression would exist for extended parental leave. But these are not society's priorities and day care is a necessity. Unfortunately, in some families, because of financial necessity, both parents need to return to work before the child is really ready to separate for a long time.

There is a big difference between day care for a child beginning after a few days or weeks post-delivery versus after a child is two and a half to three years of age. Before approximately three years of age, a child can be prone to intense distress upon being separated from a parent, usually the mother. The inner representation of the care-giving parent may not yet have been securely consolidated in the child's mind. Thus, in the presence of a need, the absent parent temporarily cannot be securely substituted by an internal image of the parent, and a child will likely experience distress. A preschool that is aware of this will arrange for parents to be present, for children three years and under, either in the classroom or in the building to be summoned if their child becomes distressed.

During the first few months of an infant's life, it is the engagements of the mother with her infant that is essential to help her infant's mind develop. It is a mother's responsiveness to her infant's upset, when her infant in need is at its most alert state having been awakened from its somnolent state because of hunger or pain, that enables the infant gradually to learn that something outside of it reduces noxious feelings. The mother takes on a significance of special importance in the surrounding external world beginning in the second half of the first year and substitutes for her will have a different way of responding to the infant. These differences can cause confusion and upset. The child's mind is not sufficiently developed to cope with the distress. In a daycare venue caregivers will be responsible for more than one infant and will be unable to show the optimal attentiveness that an infant requires especially during the earliest months. Later in the second half of the first year and early into the second year it often is only the mother that the child desires and can be comforted by, despite the best efforts by devoted daycare caregivers.

Businesses vary in terms of the length of maternal leave that they grant their female employees or temporary leave for spouses whose wives have delivered babies or have adopted a child. The longer there is financed maternal leave, the more opportunity for the mother-child attachment to establish a foothold. Some countries also provide financial assistance to their citizens to take maternal leave.

While I have a bias against day care for children younger than three years of age, based on the reasons stated above, I recognize that practical realities make it a financial necessity. In some circumstances it may not be a financial necessity for a woman but rather a practical necessity for career circumstances. Many women derive great satisfaction from their careers. Given this reality what could make day care more attuned to developmental needs of children and parents? In some countries, e.g., France, day care centers are government supported. Training to become an early educator is a respected and well-paid career. This would be helpful in the States. Undoubtedly, many caregivers who work in daycare centers are devoted and loving parent surrogates. Many, however, lack knowledge about child development, although some are parents too. Smaller care-giver/child ratios would be desirable, but insofar as the enterprise of day care is a for-profit one it would need to be economical to build more centers. Insofar as my contribution is not politically focused, let me return to the psychological issues.

Before selecting a day care center, parents best visit some if possible, and select one where the children seem happy and the workers genuinely fond of them. Notice the ratio of caregivers to children.

If a caregiver is responsible for many children, it is unlikely that any one child will get sufficient personal attention. Is there a good balance between free/structured play and cognitive learning? Parent might choose to interview the director of the day care center to learn about the model of care of children practiced.

When a young child is absent from parents, providing them with photos of them that they can access during the time spent away can be helpful. Day care workers can refer to the child's parents now and again to underscore the parents' importance. The schedule of the parent can be known and mentioned and the child can be reassured that "Mommy is at lunch now and thinking of you." On some occasions the parent can be talked to on the phone (cell phones make this more possible). Parents can visit when possible so that the venue has their imprimatur on it for their child.

The old adage, "It's the quality and not the quantity that matters," is true. Parents need to maximize the quality of time spent with their children who are in day care. One-on-one time, if practical, is desirable. Parents can observe children at home. Are they eager to go to daycare or do they protest? Are they clingier than before starting day care? Are they having trouble sleeping? In other words, parents can be alert to evidence of tension, stress and conflict. If they see such evidence, a consultation with the provider and caregiver responsible for their child can be arranged. If their observations corroborate those of the parents, it can be asked what the day care workers intend to do to make the child feel more comfortable? Collaboration between parents and the surrogate caregiver is encouraged so that a child hears complementary things to reassure them.

Chapter 7
The Oedipal Years

During the years 3-5, a major developmental change occurs, sometimes beginning as early as the latter half of the second year. In our Western traditional intact families, Oedipal themes can be observed in the interactions of the child with parents, in play, in the child's reverie, sometimes verbalized with the intention to be heard by the parent, but also often in a disguised derivative way capable of being noticed only by the trained observer. What do we mean by Oedipal themes? The term is taken from a Greek myth where Oedipus kills his father, both unaware of their relationship, and then marries his own biological mother, both also unaware of their relationship, all in accordance with a soothsayer's prescient telling of the future. Oedipus afflicts self-punishment upon himself, blinding himself, when he learns the truth. Certainly this is a monumental tragedy. For our little boy or girl, while it can be very intense, it indeed is not so tragic. Nevertheless, the Oedipal experience for a child is a major step in development.

It is a time of **powerful** emotions for the child. It is also an opportunity, metaphorically, for the child to struggle with an internal "beast," the slaying of which, or more accurately, the domestication or taming of (desire and murderous feelings), leads to the early establishment of very significant internal regulatory structures in the mind of the child. By a mental structure, I do not mean an anatomical entity but a class of mental processes that are of very long-standing duration. The duration is long enough that essentially we think of it as permanent, although not immutable. Our metaphoric beast, however, never fully relinquishes its wildness and the child will need to struggle with it again, especially during adolescence. I need to acquaint you with some theoretical concepts that psychoanalysts have so that you can appreciate the complexity of the dynamics that a child's mind is engaged in. Remember, this is universal and much of it is engaged in outside of conscious awareness. While this is a difficult time for children and parents most traverse it successfully.

The boy might tell his mother he wishes to marry her, and the girl may say the same to her father. It is important to treat this seriously and not to convey that this is cute or stupid. This will be very hurtful to the young suitor. A sensitive parent will convey appreciation for the wish and add that he or she is already married to the child's father (or mother). Their child might respond back with "Daddy can go away." The flummoxed parent might say something like "Won't you miss Daddy (or Mommy)?" The boy might say "Yes," or maybe "No." Likely, the conversation will change subject, at least for the time being.

The same scenario might be played out with dolls or in play with peers and then it might go unnoticed by the parents. Teachers, child therapists, and child analysts have observed the narrative, respectively, with students and child patients. Psychoanalysts also have heard a version of this story from countless adult patients discovering or recollecting memories from early childhood. The theme enters into much of ancient Greek epics and modern world literature too. So why is it that the narrative is often derisively dismissed by most people? My hunch is that this is because the Oedipal dynamic involves intense and taboo parenticidal and incestuous wishes and feelings from our distant past (childhood) that we all want to keep locked away in the unconscious part of our minds. Also, sexuality in particular, and drives in general, are diminished in importance as motives in generating behavior by some modern psychoanalytic theorists. I believe that this is wrong.

Let us return to our young boy and girl. The Oedipal drama involves a triangular relationship, the child and both parents. This is a mental change from a relationship with a single parent. Prior to this development the complexity of triangular relationships was beyond the cognitive capabilities of the child's mind. The mind has to deal with complicated wishes and feelings simultaneously towards the mother, father, and self. This is a lot to deal with. Also, the picture is not as straight forward as portrayed in the above-imagined conversation between the boy or girl and the parent of the opposite sex. To complicate circumstances, the parent felt to be a rival is also a parent that the child loves and needs. These are the ingredients for universal mental conflict.

Sigmund Freud was the first observer who saw the significance of the Oedipal Complex for mankind. He also accepted the scientific observation of a few contemporaries who proposed the unpopular formulation that Man is a mentally bisexual animal. Both genders are mentally inborn with a readiness to express bisexual tendencies. We refer to these traits as masculine and feminine.

For each individual there is a predominant tendency. The majority of men and women are heterosexual, but we infer each gender has a less prevalent or weaker attraction towards the same gender. After all, boys love their fathers and girls love their mothers. We infer that for boys who are dealing with Oedipal desires, the love for mother (positive Oedipal Complex) during this period is more intense than the love for father (negative Oedipal Complex) and for girls the opposite (also divided into "positive" and "negative") is true. Nevertheless, this results in the universal developmental mental conflict addressed above.

I need to expand upon the nature of the love felt for the parents during this period. It is sexual in quality. Yes, little children are not pure and innocent but have a sexual life. The sexual life of children is **different in content** from that of adults. With regard to the pleasure, however, it is the same quality, albeit of a lesser quantity. We can all observe young children touching their genitals (masturbating), not with the vigor of an adolescent, but still the same activity. The childhood notions of sex are different from that of adults. How babies are conceived is based on limited knowledge and personal bodily experiences that have had a quality of erogenous pleasure, such as eating or defecating. Theories of sex between adults are based on a child's previous experiences and misunderstandings, such as believing the moans and noises emanating behind closed parental bedroom doors as suggestive of an attack or fight between the parents. This deduction is colored by the attribution, to the imagined scenario behind closed doors, of their own sadomasochistic wishes (deriving pleasure by inflicting pain/being the recipient of pain, or controlling another person/being under another's control).

As mentioned above, children's sexual theories are based upon bodily experiences of their own, so that conception might, e.g., be based upon eating something. Children have experienced that their abdomen can get bigger after a full meal, much like a pregnant woman's belly. They may have a little scientific knowledge that can be distorted, e.g., that sperm are involved but may believe they are deposited in the mouth. They may have been told that father deposits a seed into the mother to fertilize her egg. They know that seeds develop and grow into plants. This can lead to belief that you can get pregnant if you eat something. If that is the case they too can get pregnant, regardless of their gender. They may have been told the seed comes via the father's penis. If the child is a boy, he, too, has one but all he has experienced is urine coming out of his penis. Hence, he could deduce that urination is involved in "making a baby." I think you "get the picture." Even if children have been told the facts, they prefer their own theories.

The predominant wish for the Oedipal boy is to give mother a baby and the Oedipal girl wants her father to give her a baby. But there can exist for many children a less prevalent and intense wish to have a baby with the parent of the same sex. Please keep in mind our earlier discussion, when we spoke of orality, of passive and active aims of wishes. Hence, children both want actively to produce babies for others and want passively to have babies produced in them.

The classical theoretical formulation is that for both genders the initial wish is to produce a baby with mother, with the girl switching over to the father following disappointment with the mother who is held responsible for depriving her of a penis. As mentioned earlier, this theory regarding the girl has for the most part been modified, at least with regard to the idea that the disappointment is a severe narcissistic one about not having a penis. We now know that most little girls are pleased with the genitals they have and the "inner space" (uterus) that boys do not have. Some little girls would prefer both a penis and a vagina. It is more likely, I believe, that it is the mother who is the initial figure towards whom wishes for a baby are directed because she is the predominant caregiver for girls. The girl switches to her father because of an inborn biological readiness to do so. Weaker inclinations towards the same sexed parent are present due to an inborn bisexuality.

When a boy wishes to eliminate his father, in order to have exclusive prerogatives with his mother, he becomes anxious because he believes father will retaliate. A son believes his father will become aware of his patricidal wishes. This dynamic (castration anxiety) is mostly or exclusively unconscious. Boys manifest this anxiety by frequently touching their genitals probably to reassure themselves, or by seeking reassurance by going to the bathroom supposedly to urinate, but an opportunity to handle their penis. During this phase boys (and girls) often will notice people with physical deformities in a crowd. In the mind of the boy a physical deformity is a derivative of castration anxiety. A boy is anxious even if his father is the least threatening and enlightened of fathers. This is so, we believe, because the boy unconsciously attributes to his father his own wishes to castrate his parent (to take away the source of his imagined power and prerogatives) and imagines retaliatory punishment. The boy's mind employs this mental maneuver (projection) because of the anxiety ensuing from the conflict of ambivalence between opposing loving and hating feelings directed at father. But getting rid of hostile wishes in such a manner is not very adaptive and the attempt boomerangs.

The father as rival likely originates at an earlier time, during the latter part of the oral phase when father is perceived to interrupt the physical closeness between mother and infant. We can only speculate that a father is experienced by both boy and girl infants as an intruder that interrupts the emotional intimacy with their mother. As a child matures and fantasies become more sophisticated, a fantasized elimination of the father as an intruder can be accomplished. Later in adolescence during experiences of unrequited love we wonder if this primal feeling is revived and adds to the agony of unattainable love. Primal fantasies of merging with mother are unavailable to consciousness. However, insofar as we believe that timelessness is characteristic of the Unconscious we wonder if such fantasies enter into dreams and offer some gratification to a victim of unrequited love.

The situation for the girl is more complicated. It cannot be that the loss of a penis as punishment for competitive and matricidal feelings can be a threat. Most girls have already acknowledged the absence of a penis. The loss of mother's love, however, can be a felt threat. For both sexes the discomfort can be so intense that they retreat from Oedipal dynamics.

Some children regress to earlier ways of relating. There is a tendency for children under stress to regress temporarily to earlier levels. We see it when children are tired or sick. At each earlier level of development there are vulnerable spots (fixations) because of earlier experiences that may not have been traversed smoothly and these act like magnets to draw the inner life of the child back to them. Here an observer looks "backwards" in time to understand present day behavior. Both drive expressions and ways of relating will be colored by earlier experiences. Immature ways of relating to parents and immature behaviors to obtain gratification may come to the fore. Sleeping may become disturbed as the child's dreams are immersed with the struggle that has been retreated from.

This can be a stressful time for parents and children. If handled well by parents it need not be permanent and the child can get back on a progressive course. Sometimes professional help for the family is prudent. It is also possible for a child to avoid Oedipal stress via fleeing to the next developmental level. However, if this is a result of avoidance it is unlikely it is progressive or that the child lingered long enough in the Oedipal stage to benefit from it.

An imagined threat of genital injury for a boy and loss of love for a girl, act as strong motivators to move out of the troubled waters of the Oedipal phase. Some modicum of reality intrudes and children realize with some narcissistic hurt and disappointment that they really cannot rival their parent for the exclusive love of the other parent. They realize they are children and not adults. They envy the privileges and skills of their adult parents. This is another determinant of the partial dissolution of the Oedipal Complex. I say "partial," insofar as it is doubtful that the Oedipus Complex is ever completely obliterated. Typically, both boys and girls have struggled for years with loving and hating feelings for beloved and depended-upon parents. As mentioned above, we speculate that from very early on father is experienced as an intruder interrupting the intimacy of the infant with its mother. The insidious feeling of jealousy has its primordial origin in this struggle. Because of various mental maneuvers to weaken and/or disguise demands for action made by conflicting wishes, around the end of the fifth year a child can get distance by repressing Oedipal wishes, i.e., relegating them to the unconscious part of the mind and guarding against their re-entry into conscious awareness.

Correlated with this repression is a partial identification with the parent of the same sex, the main rival and therefore potential threat. It is partial because the identification is with the conscience of the parent. So, in place of forbidden Oedipal desire for the mother, by identifying with father's superego, the male child has internalized the representation of societal moral standards, the "shalls" and "shall nots." One of the "shall nots" is a prohibition against patricidal and incestuous desires. We might say "father," in this respect, represents the demands of reality. Earlier, boys have identified with the paternal figure in what we call a masculine identification. We could say this is an early ego ideal type of identification. Ego ideals are akin to ideal selves that the child aspires to and are changeable. It is a task of late adolescence for achieving an integration of the disparate self-ideals that exist. Boys have also identified with their mothers early on. In part this might be with the "active" mother, i.e., the care-giving mother, but they also might identify with the more passive aspects of mother, what is traditionally labeled as "feminine." There is more acceptance of feminine qualities in males and masculine qualities in females, and the current generation is less threatened by transgender behavior than previous ones.

Another consequence of feeling Oedipal defeat is for the boy again to identify with his father as his ego ideal, that is, the self he would like to become. After all, father is mother's choice over him. A girl can deal with Oedipal defeat in a similar fashion. Father chose mother over her and gave mother a baby. Taking her mother as her ego ideal that she strives to be like can help her deal with her wounded narcissism as a result of feeling defeated in her oedipal strivings.

In a valued relationship with another person a likely constituent of the mental representation of the relationship is identification with the person. In an identification a self representation is modified to be like a part or the whole of an object representation. Initially there is a sameness between the self and object representation along with their drive (libido/aggression) investments. With further mental processing (internalization) a depersonification of an identification can occur, making it less personal. Thereby, an identification can be re-organized (transformed) to a different level into a mental structure that may unexpectedly enrich a child's mind. However, it is not uncommon for children to identify with whomever severely frightens them; we call this identification with the perceived aggressor. This is an instance of non-linear discontinuity in development that may become a nonenriching transformation. While identificatory processes are ongoing, object relationships continue, e.g., as with a child and its parents.

One consequence of the part identification with the conscience of the parent of the same gender for the oedipal child transitioning into Latency is that this rudimentary agency of the mind employs the very aggression and libido directed at the parents now towards the self. Thus, when the child's thoughts and/or behavior goes against moral codes, condemnatory guilt is now felt by the child; and, when the thoughts and/or behavior is in accordance with inner standards, the child feels love from his conscience. In its early state the conscience has links to the unconscious drives (wishes), which contributes to its tyrannical and absolutist quality, as well as to reality. As a child gets older, however, the conscience can become less linked to the unconscious drives (wishes) and become less rigid, more compassionate and maturely organized. This part of the mind, only rudimentary up to now, becomes like an inner policeman, an "inner helper" or moral compass to help the child control powerful drives. Insofar as it is usually the parental figures with which the Oedipal drama unfolds, they are the models whose consciences are identified with in this process of partial Oedipal Complex dissolution. If the parents are morally corrupt, these are the standards identified with by the child. Fortunately, the conscience is not immutable beyond all possibility.

Girls find it easier to identify with their mothers than do boys. Boys always are longing for maternal closeness, but are very conflicted about it. Mother's femininity is not easy for them to identify with. They may identify with aspects of mother that are active. Girls recognize mother to be the same gender and aspire to be physically like her as they mature. Her generative powers are emulated. Girls have identified with their mothers all along as ego ideals (feminine identification). Identifying with her conscience is a part of the process of dissolution for the girl of Oedipal desires for the father and matricidal urges directed at mother.

In instances where families are not intact, such as after death or divorce, or with households having single parents, Oedipal dramas can still unfold, albeit with greater difficulty. The mind of a child is very creative and the pressure brought upon it by unconscious desire is very strong. Solutions are sought and created in fantasy, if necessary. Sometimes an elder sib, an aunt or uncle, or a teacher is drawn into an imagined triangle. Of course, an imagined triangle is not as compelling as a real one, so we can expect this Oedipal narrative to be convoluted and maybe not as intense.

For children where the Oedipal Complex is not experienced, this is a disadvantage because of a reduced opportunity for progressive development of the mind, i.e., the internalized conscience. An example might be a child so engrossed in earlier pre-Oedipal issues because of a broad and strong oral fixation that Oedipal issues cannot be reached at the expected chronological age. For most children, the Oedipal Complex will be revived with puberty, and there is a second chance for children of all familial circumstances, to resolve it more thoroughly. Regrettably, a child with strong pre-Oedipal fixations will still be at a disadvantage when Oedipal issues are re-visited in adolescence. To use a metaphor of Freud's, because of the multi-fronts at which they are waging a war against conflicted oral, anal-urethral and phallic wishes, many battles will be lost and retreats will take place. There will be few, if any, troops to wage war at the Oedipal stage. Under these circumstances, the Oedipal struggle will be only a small skirmish. Some children have such massive fixations in pre-Oedipal phases that the Oedipal struggle is not engaged in by the mind. In such instances progressive developments will not be experienced. The mind will be arrested and express itself in a primitive quality devoid of moral and other regulatory restraints.

With the partial dissolution of the Oedipal Complex, a fantasy known as the family romance can be enacted in a child's play, or expressed in a dream. The theme appears in world literature, often in fairy tales.

The family romance usually has its onset during the Latency years where an educated observer can see it in derivative form in the play of children in the early stages of Latency. Sometimes this fantasy may even be in the conscious awareness of a child without an appreciation by the child of its meaning. In the family romance fantasy a child entertains the notion that he or she is not living with his or her biological parents but with adoptive parents. It seems to owe its existence to disillusionment with parents stemming from disappointment of Oedipal wishes. One's biological parents are imagined to be of a higher station, or social class, or even from royalty. In this manner, the real biological parents are devalued, insofar as Oedipal wishes have gone ungratified, and the imagined parents are idealized to deal with the narcissistic hurt.

In instances when a child really has been adopted, and is aware of this fact, the family romance fantasy is modified. A blood relationship to the adoptive parents is imagined in the fantasy. The real biological parents are imagined to have kidnapped them or that in the hospital there was a mistaken kinship assigned to them. This is an attempt to cut the tie to the real biological parents. Hence, the real biological parents are devalued to deal with the fact and resultant narcissistic hurt that they gave up the child for adoption. Adoptees who are products of open adoptions have to contend with family romance dynamics that only adds to the child's potential confusion, in addition to the other issues alluded to earlier.

Another unconscious fantasy, seen in some adult men, having its origins in disappointment in their Oedipal desires, is what we term a "rescue" fantasy. Essentially, the male imagines rescuing a "fallen" or "needy" woman (the mother in disguise who has chosen his father over him) and giving her a child like himself, thereby being his own father to himself.

The Oedipal years of their children can be very stressful for some parents. Most parents support the emancipation of their children, albeit it some with mixed feelings. Earlier, I pointed out that as a child progresses through their life and passes through phases of development, a parent's own vulnerable "hot spots" can be rekindled. If a parent experienced an intense Oedipal phase in their own childhood, they might re-experience such thoughts and feelings. A father might become competitive with his son for the attention of his wife, or make veiled castration threats to his son evoking the boy's castration anxiety. Some parents act immodestly around their children, so that nudity is commonplace. If a spouse is away, a parent might not object to an adolescent sleeping in the parental bed. Such actions are over-stimulating of children, and get them excited and usually anxious because of imagined reprisals. Adequate means of discharging the excitement are not available. As a general principle, exposing children to parental sexual intimacy should be avoided.

Censorship by parents of over-stimulating sexual and frightening violent themes in movies and on television is called for to protect children from feeling overwhelmed. They may already feel so because of inner thoughts and feelings and adding to this does not make good sense. Here parents may take a lot of "heat" because their child's friends may be allowed to watch such programs and movies. Likely, censorship will be incomplete insofar as a child may be exposed to inappropriate content in a friend's home. Perhaps a child can talk about it afterwards so parents can be of help. Here, the value of having a good communication with a child cannot be over-stated. Children whose parents endeavor to engage them in processing their confusing and scary thoughts and feelings are truly fortunate. The written word is less problematic, insofar as children can take the time to ponder and process what they are reading before going onto the next page. Literature should also be appropriate to the child's level of comprehension.

Chapter 8
Psychological disturbances of the early years of childhood

As you read this section, please keep in mind that while a parent and child may be struggling with a developmental issue or a particular behavior, we do not mean to convey necessarily that the struggle is considered pathological or that the difficulty is being elevated to a diagnosable level. Most struggles are temporary if dealt with in a reasonably appropriate manner by parents. What follows is a description of the common problems that parents become aware of from birth through the teenage years of their child. Some of these problems have their onset generally in connection with a particular stage of development but may continue into the next contiguous stage or beyond. I will try to make it clear from my exposition as to what age child I am talking about. It is beyond my focus to consider autism.

Developmental Interferences
When parents introduce expectations that are inappropriate to the developmental age of the child, i.e., where the child has not the capabilities of satisfying them, the parents are introducing a developmental interference. This can be experienced at any chronological age of childhood. The child will experience unnecessary stress. For example, over-stimulating a child and then expecting him or her to go to sleep is not an expectation that can be satisfied by the child. Or if a parent expects a fifteen-month-old toddler to be compliant with toileting expectations, this is unrealistic. If the parent gets impatient and angry it impacts the young toddler in a deleterious way. If this is

typical and happens a lot we have the potential conditions for a cumulative trauma. Single instances of this kind of inappropriate parental impatience do not seriously hurt a child but repeated ones "add up" and can result in trauma. When a single instance of a very unpleasant experience is so severe it is traumatic, an experience we label as a shock trauma.

Earlier, we defined trauma as an experience where a person feels unprepared and overwhelmed to deal efficiently with the amount of stimuli impinging upon the mind. Such experiences have negative consequences for a child in its ability to regulate feelings, among other things. When traumatized, children usually display behavior indicative of a significant disruption of psychic equilibrium. Later in this chapter we will discuss what we mean by developmental conflict, psychoneurosis, and delinquency.

Sleep Problems

Usually, the first manifestation of a "problem" that parents encounter is difficulty putting a young baby to sleep. Parents become very stressed about this for two reasons. Firstly, they believe correctly that the child needs to sleep for its wellbeing. Secondly, the baby's sleeping is a respite for the parents to attend to their own chores and needs, including sleeping or grabbing a nap. Infants differ as to their degree of fussiness. Some are easy to satisfy and seem to naturally and almost seamlessly fall into rhythms of sleeping and being awake. But others seem to find this rhythm impossible to achieve. Some infants suffer from colic and seem to be inconsolable and impossible to fall asleep (see Chapter 2). By trial and error, parents hope to find the panacea that will allow them to overcome future periods of difficulty in this arena. For the most part, the majority of children eventually fall into a cycle (usually by six months) that fits into their family's life style. But problems of sleep will arise again and again, usually temporarily. Sleeping seems to be a bodily activity prone to disruption during periods of stress. As adults we know that to be true. Also, as a child progresses through different developmental stages the issues of each particular stage can contribute toward sleeping disruptions, e.g., a child struggling with toilet mastery can be afraid of soiling while asleep.

A major problem is when parents react to temporary disruptions in ways that could lend the problem to become a permanent one. Parents are not "bad" if they become impatient with a child that will not easily fall asleep. It can be difficult for all parents. To lighten things up, I will introduce a bit of humor into a distressing topic. I will tell you of a _New Yorker_ cartoon on the subject. It shows a husband and wife in bed bandaged up to look like mummies. The caption is, "This should keep Emily from running to our bed every time she has a bad dream." Obviously, this strategy is not advised.

A more pernicious problem is when parents' marital problems get played out in a child's bedroom. It is not uncommon for spouses that are unhappy with each other and avoiding sexual intimacy to exacerbate their child's sleeping problems, e.g., by not conveying clear expectations that their child sleep through the night and not come into the parental bedroom. Another issue is the transgenerational transmission of trauma. For example, a parent as a young child may have been exposed to his or her own parents engaged in sexual intercourse (primal scene) and traumatized because of the misinterpretation of the scene as a violent one with one parent inflicting harm onto the other. When grown up the parent, unwittingly, i.e., unconsciously, could arrange for his or her own child to witness the same act. This child can be traumatized and a sleep problem could ensue.

When someone of any age intends to go asleep he or she are essentially disengaging from the outer world and withdrawing into the inner world. I am describing this in a subjective way. If this is valid, it does not make sense for daddy to come home from work and to stimulate his baby in a vigorous playful way and for the parents then to expect a seamless transition to sleep. We are sympathetic to the father who takes the first opportunity of his day to be playful with his newborn, but it is not in the best interests of the child that the play be vigorous or a long duration. Infants need their sleep and to postpone it until after the 11 p.m. television news is not in a baby's best interest. My impression is that infants and children of all ages stay up too late, because parents find it easier not to deal with it. Eventually, out of exhaustion, the child falls asleep. What about the benefits of allowing a baby to discover a way to sooth him or herself and put itself to sleep? Insofar as infants benefit from routine, as discussed earlier, parents need to create reliably the best possible conditions required to promote falling asleep for their infant.

It is not unusual after a family vacation in which sleeping arrangements often are not typical, for young child to have some sleep difficulties. Such problems ordinarily are temporary if parents can help the child process recent events. They understand that the vacation sleeping arrangements deviated from the usual routine and may have been scary or over-stimulating for their child, especially if the family slept together in the same room or even in the same bed.

Putting an infant to sleep, beneficially, is a moment of quiet bonding between a mother and baby, especially if breastfeeding. It's an opportunity for gazing at each other, to sing a bedtime lullaby, for bodily contact, and other warm fuzzy things. I do not advise getting into bed alongside the baby for reasons already stated. Older children like to be read to or to be told a story in bed prior to going to sleep. Parents can select an appropriate non-scary book from the vast literature or make up a story. If a story is made up, choose fictitious people so as to allow for distance to enable a child to listen. The story can include a theme of the day's experience and can include resolution of an experience that was trying for the child. Helping child to process the day's events that may not have been assimilated is useful. Otherwise, the event could enter a young child's dream.

Dreams of an upsetting nature can disrupt a child's sleep. We believe that dreams serve the purpose of wish fulfillment. Many of these wishes are not acceptable to the conscious mind. The mind of a neonate is not mature enough to dream in this fashion. We do not confidently know what constitutes a newborn's dream. A preschooler likely dreams much like an adult but some dreams are likely re-experiencing the events of the day that were intense and not processed. The more mature mind disguises a wish sufficiently so that it can get past the mind's sleeping censorship and be expressed in the dream and gain partial gratification. When the disguise has not been sufficient, and the mind's censor has caught enough of its presence in the dream to become alert, the dreamer can awake with a fright. This is a so-called "nightmare." Other nightmares are simply the inclusion in a dream of a frightening image. Parents will be alerted, either by a cry, footsteps, or pleas, "Mommy (daddy), wake up!"

Comforting will follow and putting the child back to sleep will be necessary. Expediency will dictate allowing the child to crawl into bed with a parent. Even though inconvenient, parents are advised to take the child back to their own bed and sit alongside them until they are consoled enough to go back to sleep. In the morning parents can give the child an opportunity to speak about the dream if recalled. Children can be reassured that a dream is not real. Learning the difference between pretend and real is acquired gradually and likely is attained securely by the five year old or earlier by a precocious child. A scary dog is not hiding under the bed and monsters and ghosts do not exist. If the nightmare's content is remembered and involves a frightening theme parents can help them to understand it within the limits of their cognitive capacities and psychological readiness. Here the parents' intuitive grasp of their child's readiness to process upsetting experiences will serve them well.

It is the rare child, fortunately, that walks while asleep, oblivious to safety concerns and hard to console because they are still asleep. Professionals know little about sleepwalking, and can offer little comfort to parents, except to underscore the need to secure their child's safety, e.g., putting a gate at the top of the stairs. Sleepwalking, however, usually does not become a permanent feature when it occurs.

A word should be mentioned about the faulty connection made by some children between death and sleeping. To a child, both resemble each other. If a child views a dead relative in an open-coffin memorial service the dead person will appear to the child to be asleep. Unfortunately, some parents may even compare being dead to being asleep. This erroneous explanation connects up being dead with the natural state of sleeping. It could cause falling asleep to be scary to a child. A child can be informed that when one is dead one has no feelings whatsoever evermore, but when one is asleep one is alive and does feel and wakes up refreshed.

Separation Problems

Separation issues are ubiquitous in childhood. Indeed, they underlay sleeping problems. The youngster temporarily must withdraw his emotional investment in the parent(s) and turn it inward in order to fall asleep. For some children this is difficult because of an insecure attachment to their parent(s). Contemporary psychoanalysis has identified the different types of attachment that young children are able to establish with maternal figures. We have underscored the ingredients that help secure a secure attachment. Most mothers are aware of making eye contact, not being intrusive, being in rhythm emotionally, modulating the intensity of their affect, reflecting on their child's affects and moods, etc, all of which contribute to a secure attachment with their infant. There are many empirical studies detailing the consequences for different types of attachment upon the relationship between a child and parent, as the child gets older. The bonding or attachment experience starts from day one but its consolidation is not achieved probably until 3 years of age. These principles of development were discussed earlier (see Chapters 2, 4 & 5) when we talked of the experience of "being with" involving emotional attunement, and the gradual consolidation of the capacity to maintain an internal image of the maternal figure, the one who is comforting and need satisfying, in the presence of a strong need, or a gratified need, but in the absence of that figure. We call that capacity object constancy. "Object" because it is not the self ("subject") and "constancy" because of its permanency. It is a real achievement the first time the child is able to manage a sleepover at a friend's house. This is so, even if the child insists on taking along their transitional object. Children able to do so feel securely attached and bonded with their parent(s).

As every parent knows, young children often can be clingy and react with upset when baby-sitting arrangements are made until they become familiar with the baby-sitter. Parents, understandably, are hesitant to arrange to have baby-sitters that are not relatives because of fears of the person's suitability, unless they have thoroughly vetted the person. Assuming the person is safe, it's a good idea for children to become comfortable with people other than members of their nuclear family. Of course, parents help children to be wary of strangers, whom they have not vetted, in unfamiliar settings. Probably this caution should begin when your child is a toddler.

Hospitalization of a child involves a separation in the context of pain and discomfort. Your young child's resources will be greatly taxed. This is an occasion where a parent must insist that they be with a child twenty–four hours a day as long as the child is an inpatient. Most hospitals are sophisticated about the psychological needs of ill children and their parents to know the correctness of this request and they grant it. Hospitals were not always this accommodating.

Parents wonder at what age they can have an extended vacation without the children? Usually, arrangements are made with a relative, like grandparents, to look after the children. It is preferable that the relatives temporarily move into the child's residence so that the child need not have to deal with unfamiliar surroundings at the same time as dealing with their parents' absence. This is more important the younger the child. For many children, by three years of age such a separation is viable. A stable inner representation of the parent usually has been achieved, enabling them to tolerate their parents' absence as long as their needs generally are satisfied. For many children, the upset follows their parents' return. This may appear counter-intuitive to the parents. It is as if they mobilized their defenses while the parents were gone but with their reappearance they can let down their guard. It is also a way of "paying back the parents." Yes, children can be vengeful, making their parents feel what they felt.

The ultimate separation, of course, follows the death of a parent. Professionals used to think that children were unable truly to grieve until adolescence when the natural tendency is to disengage from one's parents. Observations, however, suggest that even young children can mourn and can accept a substitute parental caregiver who satisfies their basic biological needs. With time they can bond with the substitute, too.

Toilet Mastery

Parents can pick up indications of readiness on the part of their child to begin the process of toilet mastery. Such readiness can begin from around two years onwards. Do not expect, however, that such readiness means that older toddlers necessarily will achieve toilet mastery quickly. Expressions of curiosity may occur about the toilet or about the toileting activities of their parents. There might be a spoken wish to be "like" mommy or daddy when it comes to using the toilet. Some children let you know they are ready because they become squeamish about messes and wish to have their bodies, especially their hands, clean. They may object to eating finger-foods because they dislike dirtying their fingers. They may express a desire to wear pull-ups or underwear instead of diapers.

At the beginning of toilet mastery a child-size portable toilet can be introduced. Children feel more secure if their feet touch the floor than if they dangle. Many children have a fearful approach to the toilet. They are afraid of falling into the toilet, the sound of the flush scares them, and disappearance of the stool makes them anxious. Parents need to be patient, supportive and reassuring.

After awhile, a child presents their bowel movements as "gifts" to the parent. It is experienced as part of him or herself and it is confusing when a parent seems so pleased that a child has deposited it in the toilet but then flushes it away. An explanation that everyone disposes of stools in this manner may remove the self-reference for your child. The focus should be on the child's self control over their body's products, its feces, expressing pride in the child's own achievement. Because the aim is mastery and not training, I propose not to begin toilet mastery till the toddler is at least two-and-a-half years old. Sphincter control is likely not mature at least until that age. Sometimes younger children can be toilet-trained but it is not mastery and instead it is a stimulus-response behavior.

A minority of children fails to become toilet mastered, even up to around puberty. Some children may have achieved and then lost toilet mastery. These children have a condition known as encopresis. These children soil their underpants and hide them. Soiling may occur because they try to withhold their feces but then fail to do so. Assuming there are no physical reasons, e.g., problems with the integrity of the sphincter, the causes can be multiple due to psychological conflict. The dynamics underlying the condition, e.g., could be due to an attempt to hold onto and control mother, symbolically by holding onto feces that become concrete representations of her. Consultation with a professional is warranted if a child is five years old and still soiling.

Bladder control in the daytime is usually achieved before night-time control. Sometimes the latter is accomplished but then control is lost during a time of stress and later regained. Wetting at night can sometimes be prolonged in duration. If a child is still wetting by age six (enuresis), I suggest a consultation with a professional. If nocturnal bladder control has been achieved but then lost because of acute stress the prognosis is more favorable than if it has never been achieved. When lack of bladder control extends over years, the psychological meaning of the inability to control this body function can take on additional individual meaning specific to each developmental phase it extends into. This multiple meaning is what complicates the prognosis insofar as to eliminate the symptom all of the meanings may need to be processed by the child.

The advent of nighttime pull-ups that now allow for absorbency but discomfort being wet should help. Children may wish to regulate the body function more effectively once they are physically uncomfortable from being wet. Most children know the negative social consequences of wetting, especially diurnal wetting, and make efforts to deal with it. Soiling among older children is more rare and may unconsciously have to do, as mentioned above, with the stool being treated like a person that a child wishes, concretely, to hold onto because of an insecure attachment. Parents can be reassured that almost all children will have achieved bladder and bowel control by the time puberty is reached. This late age may offer little consolation to most parents.

Eating Problems

Eating difficulties seem to be a common concern of parents. With the newborn, breastfeeding, if chosen, can be a difficulty for some women. For some women, nipples can hurt, baby's sucking response may be weak, and milk production may be minimal. We have discussed the issues coloring a decision to nurse or bottle-feed. Weaning and how and when to do it needs to be considered. The child may communicate a readiness to wean by showing less interest in the breast or bottle. Often, getting bit on the nipple becomes a motivator for the mother to consider weaning, as the child's teeth start to erupt and interest grows in more solid foods.

In our culture, nursing rarely extends beyond a year and a half in duration. Mothers become embarrassed when a two or three year old publicly asks to nurse. There are some mothers who are very insistent on the benefits of extended periods of breastfeeding. This is based, in our culture, on the psychological advantages for mother and baby, and less so for nutritional gains. There are groups such as La Leche that advocate for the practice. My own observation is that in many instances it is extended more for the mother's needs than for the child's. A major difficulty is that the mother's breast is not the best venue for the resolution of anger directed at mother once a child gets teeth.

When children enter the period when toilet mastery is starting, certain foods are avoided that can remind them of their body products. They do not like the color or dislike touching the food. They are beginning to erect defenses against a natural interest in their eliminated body products and this tendency generalizes to things that are similar in looks. Becoming clean is a conflicted goal so touching finger food can become conflictual. Use of utensils will take time to master. It's a good idea to let children "mess" with their food earlier, during their first two years, insofar as pleasure doing so can reinforce pleasure in eating and interest in foods.

There are more and more reports of eating disorders among school age children, especially among girls, a problem of endemic proportions among adolescent girls and young adult females in our culture. There is so much emphasis in the media on a standard of slimness for women, especially, that girls become very conscious of their weight. They diet to an extreme causing a psychophysiological condition called anorexia nervosa. Sometimes the eating disorder takes on the characteristic of binge eating followed by purging, what is called bulimia. Both are much more prevalent in adolescence and I will discuss the topic again later in Chapter 15.

School age kids can become vegetarian or vegans, usually temporarily, but for some, the beginning of a life choice, especially if reinforced by parental inclinations. More commonly, children develop food fads and/or food avoidances. It is common for children to dislike vegetables, much to the consternation of parents. Eating a balanced meal becomes a family creed and many a family meal can be an unpleasant experience for all when the child refuses some foods despite parental admonishments.

Eating habits are established early in life. Parents need not pressure children to eat. They should provide healthy foods and let their toddler self-regulate what he or she consume. It may take a child as much as twenty times to eat a particular kind of food before they decide they like it. Parents can have confidence that a child ultimately will eat in a growth promoting way. Parents can encourage adventurousness about what can be eaten but not insist upon it. What one tries to avoid is a power struggle. Children will always win to no one's benefit. All that struggles promote are children choosing to eat only a limited range of foods. Parents should not be expected to prepare a different meal for each child. But parents can plan menus that take into account the different tastes of children compared to adults. That way every meal will be more acceptable to all concerned. When it is not a family meal, it makes sense to prepare macaroni and cheese rather than cordon bleu. Parents can be reassured that most children broaden their tastes as they get older.

Parents are models for their children. If they overeat, eat unhealthy foods, and buy "junk food," it is likely that their children will copy them. This may be one determinant for the presence of an increase in obesity in children.

Learning Problems

Parents want their children to do well in school. This is the foundation for later achievement and competence. Teachers are much more aware these days that children differ as to learning styles. Underachievement, in some instances, in the past may have been the result of educational expectations that children conform to a method of teaching incompatible with their learning style. In such circumstances children get bored. This recognition makes teaching more difficult but modern teachers are being trained to accommodate their methods to the broader range of learning styles. While this makes intuitive sense, and experienced teachers espouse the existence of different learning styles among children, the evidence from empirical research does not support this viewpoint. The latest research suggests that varying the type of material to be learned results in a more lasting effect on the brain. It is like providing more neural connections for the material. An analogy would be an athlete mixing strength, speed and skill exercises in his or her workouts. It seems to me, however, that motivation to learn would be greater if the learner experienced the learning via a sensory mode believed to be a strength rather than a weakness. Thus, it would appear that the jury is still out on this.

Many elementary school aged children are given the diagnosis of ADD or ADHD, which connote, respectively, attention deficit and attention deficit/hyperactivity disorders. These children are then put on stimulant drugs that have a paradoxical effect, namely, they seem to calm the recipient. My own impression is that these diagnoses have been over applied and too many children have been put on a drug regimen whose long-term side effects are unknown. I believe that inattention and hyperactivity describe behaviors that can have different underlying causes. Professionals have not made these distinctions enough. Presumably, there are some children with such behaviors whose central nervous systems are functioning abnormally to cause these disruptive behaviors. These children benefit from a drug like Ritalin. I contend, however, that a majority of these disruptive children are manifesting these behaviors because they are anxious or that their particular learning styles are being ignored. For those children who are anxious, supportively listening to them may be sufficient, and if not, then psychotherapy and not drugs, may be more potent. For those who are bored or disregarded by educational methods, then a master teacher consulting to the classroom teacher might be the answer. Drugs are expedient and are not a good model, except as a last resort, for children in a culture where recreational drug taking is commonplace.

Sibling Rivalry

I was not sure under which section to put my thoughts on sibling rivalry. This was partly because it is so ubiquitous. It also can be life long, so it could be addressed under different age periods. Siblings have only one set of parents and they do not usually like sharing them. If you are an only child you may be wondering why is this so. As an only child you have wished, maybe even cajoled your parents to have another child. You have thought it would be great to have a playmate and a lifetime companion and friend who has shared common experiences. There is truth to these sentiments. It is also true, in families with more than a single child, that a sibling has likely harbored, not necessarily consciously, rivalrous thoughts and maybe even wishes to get rid of another. Siblings often think the other receives preferred treatment from a parent.

While this belief may be greatly exaggerated, it often can have some truth. Parents like to believe that they love all of their children equally and maybe consciously they do, although I do not know how you can quantify this to prove or disprove the assertion. In any case, unwittingly a parent may have feelings and thoughts about a child that may not have originated with that child but instead with someone from their own past. This phenomenon is called transference and is universal. It happens with everyone in our lives. You may, for example, transfer feelings originating with a parent or sibling onto your boss. Hence, parents do treat each child somewhat differently. Recognizing this, parents can make deliberative efforts to try to be fair.

One sib may envy another's being older, taller, having blue eyes, being more slender, wearing teeth braces, developing breasts earlier, and so on and on. Or the focus could be on talents or athletic skills, or on intelligence for academics, or on social skills and so on and on. Envy breeds resentment and wishes to sabotage. Competitiveness between siblings will not necessarily vanish in future decades as they age. Emulation, however, is also possible. A sib can vow to be just like an admired other sib in some respect.

Extended family dynamics are often dominated by sibling rivalries that extend over many years in duration. These feelings may be just beneath the surface but are able to ignite at extended family gatherings, e.g., the legendary reunions at a Christmas dinner or after the funeral of a family member. It is not uncommon for siblings to fight over the disbursement of family heirlooms, memorabilia, furniture, etc., after both parents are deceased.

How are parents to deal with sibling rivalry? I think that first they have to recognize it and acknowledge it. Parents can endeavor to be fair and this may considerably reduce sibling rivalry, especially among older sibs who have acquired some insight. In my view, being fair does not mean providing the same for each child or arranging the same enrichment for each child. Each child is an individual with unique needs, skills and talents. Children are capable of recognizing this reality and are able to appreciate parents doing so, too. But being fair in setting limits, showing affection, disciplining, and so on, may not be perceived to be so, despite a parent's best efforts. As the children get older they can be encouraged to settle their differences directly with each other, and not use a parent as an intermediary. Some children will gravitate towards one parent to try to get them to support their grievance and get them as an advocate to lobby on their behalf with the other parent in family disputes. Spouses can avoid this and present a united position in many instances. They can, at least, agree that the older children settle their differences directly with one another.

Developmental Conflicts

A developmental conflict is unavoidable and even can be beneficial for a child because of the growth promoting consequences of a successful struggle with the conflict. An example of this kind of conflict is the Oedipal Complex, discussed in Chapter 7. Its reappearance in later developmental phases, discussed below, reintroduces conflict and another growth promoting opportunity. Childhood is a time of many fears, but these are not disorders. They are a result of limited cognitive abilities of a child to understand an experience or maybe even inborn in some instances. They are usually temporary and respond well to clarifications and explanations offered by an adult. Fears of thunder, e.g., may be inborn and have to do with evolutionary genetics. Phobias, on the other hand are fears that are part of so-called psychoneuroses.

Psychoneuroses

Psychoneuroses are symptoms that result from maladaptive resolutions of mental conflict. Sometimes they are transitory and/

or stage (phase)-limited, although sometimes psychoneuroses can endure over a number of years. I need to present some theory here. These conflicts occur within the mind when competing and contradictory demands are made upon it. Originally, conflict was between the child and the parent as representative of the external world. The wish for candy causes a demand (in our model) to be made upon the mind to act in order to satisfy this desire. A parent may thwart a child's desire for candy. This is an external conflict. After many similar interactions, a representation of a prohibiting parent is internalized. Now conflict can be between the wish for candy and the internalized representation of the prohibiting parent. We call the collection of prohibitory images the conscience. The child's mind (in our model, specifically the executive part) will feel anxious, and must mediate between desire and internal and/or external prohibition. The solution, in our example, might be for the child to secretly stash candy away and consume it when the parent is absent and later to feel guilty, or consume it if the conscience can be seduced into leniency by a rationalization. Or the child might never again eat candy. All these solutions can become symptomatic and are maladaptive and neurotic. This simplified example is what we mean by neurotic conflict.

"One-shot" instances usually do not result in neurotic conflict except if traumatic. The prerequisites for the formation of a neurosis require sufficient mental structures, as illustrated in Chapter 5 in our model of neurotic conflict. Recall, a mental structure is a collection of mental processes of unlimited duration of existence. An example of a structure would be a mental agency such as the conscience. When psychoanalysts use the term symptom we mean a behavior that is a compromise between a wish and a defense. In other words, a symptom is the compromise between a wish and adherence to the constraints of reality (as represented by an internal regulatory structure). The symptom when analyzed contains elements traceable back to the components of the neurotic conflict, namely, wish, defense, and usually guilt. You can decipher these in the behavior of a child who secretly stores candy. The development of psychoneuroses requires that at least the phallic-oedipal phase has been reached.

There are different kinds of classes of psychoneuroses based on typical dynamics [conflicts] and symptoms, e.g., phobias, anxiety hysteria, hysterical conversions, anxiety disorders, and obsessive-compulsive symptoms. In childhood, psychoneuroses are often mixed, i.e., having symptoms reflective of conflict from different levels. Insofar as my focus is not on psychopathology, I will present descriptions of the different neuroses in a brief manner.

In phobias, a classical example would be an anxiety that a particular kind of experience will result in injury or death. Analysis will reveal that the fear of death is symbolic of injury to the body, in concrete terms, castration. The thing imagined to cause the injury is a displacement from a significant figure, e.g., father. So a boy may fear horses that will bite him, instead of father injuring his genitals. In anxiety hysteria there is a repression of Oedipal wishes in an attempt to avoid conflict. The mind is unsuccessful despite employment of phobic or obsessive defenses. The mind of the child remains apprehensive that repressed wishes will return to consciousness and anxiety can be intense. If repression has to be assiduously maintained it can spread and a pseudo-stupidity can result as a symptom. In hysterical conversion, there is also repression of Oedipal wishes and ensuing conflict, as the mind converts the conflict mainly to a somatic symptom. Abdominal pains can be a symbolic hysterical equivalent of labor pains resulting from a girl's competitive wishes towards a pregnant mother. In an anxiety neurosis there is a free floating anxiety that may at times feel like panic. In obsessive-compulsive neurosis, Oedipal wishes and fantasies are not acceptable to the conscious mind, causing guilt and anxiety. There is a regression to an anal-sadistic level and this augments the guilt already felt. Magical thinking, characteristic of the mind during the early years, along with a whole host of defenses is employed, resulting in the obsessional and compulsive symptoms. An example might be a child who has to rearrange the bed's pillows repeatedly before being able to go to sleep. If the child does not "get it right" he or she will feel anxious. Presumably, the arrangement has to be a perfect and specific as a way to ward off some imagined dreaded event. In neurotic depression, depressive feelings are reactive to events like a disappointment or loss (e.g., a separation or ending of a relationship).

These feelings are not thought to have a biological etiology. The depressive feelings can be accompanied by anxiety. In many instances unconscious guilt feelings underlie the depressive feelings. An important dynamic is an unconscious symbolic meaning of the experienced loss. For example, a person might get a job promotion but become depressed because they have lost a less desirable position, which satisfied a need to be punished for perceived Oedipal triumph. You can see that the evolution of psychoneuroses often involves Oedipal dynamics.

A type of dynamic therapy, e.g., child psychoanalysis, is the treatment of choice for these disturbances. Parental involvement is part of this intervention. Such interventions can be of great help. Parents need to insure that they are referred to a properly trained child analyst. I will discuss this further in Chapter 22.

Delinquency

Delinquency describes behavior that is due to a poorly consolidated inner morality, or conscience, or the consequence of one that is modeled on sociopathic adults. Healthy guilt cannot be utilized to help regulate urges. The delinquent child takes whatever he or she wants without feeling guilt or later contrition. Their only regret is getting caught. Sometimes such behavior can look delinquent but the underlying cause may be an attempted resolution of a mental conflict, i.e., the child may be seeking to be punished as a neurotic compromise between desire and prohibition (neurotic delinquency). We will say more about this when we discuss adolescence.

Super-Intelligence

It may seem counter-intuitive to you that such a section is included in a chapter dealing with early childhood disturbances. Being very intelligent ordinarily is considered an asset, but, regretfully, it can include a particular risk. In the case of **very** intelligent children, a keen precocious social awareness can occur before the mind is developed sufficiently to be able to regulate intense drives and feelings. Because of their sharp awareness, these children are very sensitive to nuances of social judgment that less intelligent children ordinarily are unaware of. I am thinking here about normal exuberant, noisy and crude behavior of young children that many adults can find intrusive and unacceptable. A potential consequence for these children is to experience external disapproval. They begin to have an expectation of disapproval and a general inhibition can result. They will not be able to capitalize on their keen intelligence in the interest of social adaptation and will be awkward in relating to others. Some of these children in school resort to clowning as a neurotic maneuver to disarm imagined disapproving peers or adults. Sensitive parenting can be very helpful to such a child. Parents can help these children to use their keen intelligence to process their feelings.

The opposite sort of imbalance is also possible. That is, some children who are very intelligent may have precocious egos demonstrated in creative and imaginative fantasying, advanced understanding of the external world, but their internal ego controls and "inner policeman" (conscience) may be delayed, perhaps because of the inability of their parents to set limits. Such children may have difficulties in impulse control and could have difficulties in complying with classroom expectations of decorum.

Chapter 9
Latency

Latency for the majority of children extends roughly from age six through ten. Hence, it coincides with entry into primary school and ends with the advent of the earliest signs of puberty, what we term the "preadolescent years." The term latency is meant to convey that the powerful drives or urges of the preceding years, especially the Oedipal years, have receded and their power *vis-à-vis* the executive part of the mind, have been diminished. While the balance of power has shifted, it is not true that the latency child can "forget about" sexual and aggressive wishes throughout latency. One only has to observe boys touching their genitals, what has been felicitously termed "pocket pool," to appreciate that sexual (libidinal) drives do not disappear, or to see the meanness of a group of latency age girls against a peer that has been banished from the group to recognize that aggression also has not expired. This biphasic development of the ascendency and retreat of the strength of drives is uniquely human.

The role of the Latency Period of development is to consolidate gains and prepare the child (the mind) for the onslaught of puberty. That is, with puberty, the drives strengthen in power and are once again in ascendancy vis-à-vis the part of the mind that directs executive functioning (e.g., judgment, reasoning, etc.), the negotiator between the inner and outer worlds. With puberty, maturation of the genitals and reproductive system takes place and genital drives demand to be gratified. With puberty, such drives can potentially be discharged and gratified in mature ways, unlike earlier in age. However, drives from earlier phases, what are termed pre-genital ones, the oral, anal, urethral, and phallic drives, are also strengthened and clamor for expression. This renewed strength of the drives threatens the defenses set up against their expression. So, the mind of the pubertal child has to have been reinforced in its defenses and coping skills *vis-à-vis* the drives during latency to withstand the surge of drives in puberty.

By withstanding we essentially mean for the mind to have developed a resistance to regression. Under the pressure of the drives, the child (the mind) could succumb to the expression of less mature ways of gratifying them if the executive part of the mind was not reinforced. The strengthening of the conscience is another attainment of the latency years. Recall, it was internalized in a more completed manner, reinforcing a primitive conscience, at the time of the dissolution of the Oedipal Complex, resulting in entry into the Latency Phase. Together, the executive component of the mind and the conscience, ally themselves against the strengthened drives of puberty. It is analogous to the strengthening of levees after a strong hurricane that breached them so that hopefully this will not happen again when another even stronger hurricane occurs.

The standards of groups that latency age children affiliate with help support the internalized but still relatively weak conscience. Groups such as the Cub Scouts, Brownies, athletic teams, can provide a code of ethics and standards of sportsmanship that help to strengthen the conscience. Children engage in competitive games and are very cognizant of the rules of the game that they adhere to, so that cheating is frowned upon. During the latency years religious training may also begin for some children and this, too, strengthens the immature "inner helper" of early childhood. Educational efforts in school also encourage ethical choices.

With the relative weakening of the drives, the mind can pay more attention to reality and mastery over it. Latency is a time to focus on and learn about the world. Around age eight there is a significant change in the formal properties of thinking, from immature to more mature. It is no wonder that the beginning of formal education coincides with entering Latency for most children. Amassing knowledge about the world allows children to feel more comfortable outside of their nuclear family. Adults that are not relatives, such as teachers, librarians, coaches, clergy, can be related to. Further information about the world can be imparted to young minds and thereby expanding their familiarity with the world even further. However, latency age children continue to identify with aspects of their parents in various ways. Via identification (internalization) they broaden their repertoire of interests and skills and thereby enrich the strength and competency of their egos. Latency age children are eager to learn.

The development of practical skills and comfort engaging the world outside the boundaries of the family all contribute to a sense of competency. This feeling about oneself is a great asset that contributes to feelings of self-worth, self-esteem, and self-reliance. The image of oneself as competent will help one recover quickly from feelings of helplessness which are unavoidably experienced at various times in a lifetime. That one basically feels they can be reliant on one's own inner resources will help, not hinder, asking for help when needed.

Speech and language are utilized a great deal by latency age children. Sometimes speech is used more to hide and shield than to communicate, e.g., outright lying, or the use of "pig Latin" with initiated friends to exclude others, and the use of text messaging with its encryption among modern preteens and teenagers. But speech is mainly used to communicate to others one's feelings, inner thoughts, knowledge, organizational plans, etc. There is less use of the body to express feelings and a greater reliance on words to label and articulate feelings. There continues to be less use of action to communicate. Fantasy, an organized narrative, is distinguished from rational thought during these years. Nevertheless, belief in magic, the power of thoughts, can still be strong. For example, a latency age child will chant the admonishment "step on a crack, break your mother's back," although in jest, nevertheless conveying its power. Fantasy is most often unconscious, distinguishing it from daydreams.

We encourage our children to use their words, but sometimes beginning with latency, children use curse words and adults become upset about this. They are discovering that some words have a power that can upset adults. Of course, if parents use these words, it should not surprise them that their children will imitate them. I think if a parent reacts in a calm way these words can be demystified and reduce the shock value of them for the child. The task is to clarify that the "f word" has been subverted from connoting a private activity involving love, intimacy, and pleasure between two consenting adults to one involving coercion and violence, thereby becoming insulting and derogatory. This may seem to be a daunting task (see Chapter 11 for suggestions about sex education) but remember that children can comprehend more than we give them credit for. I think that the child is partly experimenting with the power of words, having observed that such words are provocative. This is a good opportunity for parents to have a meaningful discussion with their child about social awareness and social manners, crudity versus civility, catharsis versus articulate verbal expression, forgivable transgressions versus punishable ones, etc. The discussion by parents with their child need not be complicated. It can include an explanation of the social effects of using these words. In most instances the value of these words to get adults upset will dwindle away. We should encourage our children to express their angry feelings without being disrespectful.

The achievement of rational thinking does not come easy. The latency age child can still believe in magic and accept correlation as causation, especially when anxious or fearful. I am reminded of a joke about two nine-year old boys who are sharing a hospital room. They ask each other what operation each is undergoing the next day. One says a tonsillectomy and the other recalls how great it was after he had that procedure at age four to be able to eat all the ice cream he desired post-operatively. The other indicates he is having a circumcision. The other boy says that is not so great. After his at 8 days old he could not walk for a year!

In creative activities, like in the arts and drama, regression when controlled by the ego can be very useful. It can allow the artist, playwright, or actor to be creative. Latency age children can become very interested in creative expression. There is a suspension of reality testing during fantasying. Both regression in the service of the ego and fantasying allow for the magic of the unconscious to imbue the rationality of the ego with a sense of wonder that vitalizes our experiences. But, during creating art or witnessing an artistic event and engaging in fantasy the mind (ego) does not abandon its allegiance to reality.

The use of mental processes to control drive expressions through suppressing, inhibiting, and modifying is relied upon during the latency years. The armamentarium of these mental processes, called defenses, is expanded. Some of the more prominent ones are repression, isolation of affect, displacement, projection, externalization, and reaction formation. In repression the mental representation of a forbidden idea or feeling is kept securely out of conscious awareness. In isolation of affect only the idea can enter conscious awareness, not the connected feeling. In displacement, a recipient is chosen who is different but linked to the intended recipient of a conflicted drive expression. In projection one unconsciously attributes a conflicted wish to someone else and then consciously claims the recipient is directing the wish at him or her. In externalization one attributes an unwanted aspect of one's own self-image to another person. In reaction formation one is aware only of a feeling opposite to one unconsciously felt towards another, e.g., awareness of loving feelings and not hating feelings. There are numerous other defenses. While named defenses are frequently used, **any** mental process can be utilized by the mind (supported by its conscience) as a defense against an unacceptable thought and/or feeling.

Some learning difficulties in children are due to the secondary interference of defenses. For example, if a child needs to squelch their sexual curiosity, for whatever reason, curiosity in general may suffer and this would affect learning. Or if a child needs to deny a painful reality, links between aspects of the denied reality to other components of reality will be disconnected and this could affect learning. When a topic is repressed from consciousness, associative links may not be readily available to memory and affect learning. Such learning disorders have a neurotic etiology.

Latency is a time period when sexual (libidinal) or aggressive drives can have their respective, erotic and destructive, aims modified to more socially acceptable ones. Exhibitionistic display in contemporary fashion is an acceptable erotic expression, as long as it does not go over an acceptable line. Athletics is an activity where aggression can be expressed in forms that society does not punish nor try to induce guilt about. In football, for example, a fearsome tackle is applauded, not condemned. Through various hobbies, collections, and interests, derivative drive expressions can be invested in without social disapprobation. The psychoanalysis of people of all ages indicates that such endeavors owe their origin to erotic or aggressive drives where the aims were successfully transformed (sublimated or de-aggressivized) beginning in latency. Hobbies of all kinds engage children during these years and often are sustained during the whole life span. Musical and dance skills often begin and success seems to be based on inborn talent, an asset that not all children possess. If a child has a passion for music or dance he or she will not need to be pressured to practice. Athletic success also seems to be based on inborn talent.

I do not advocate coercing children to practice. I do suggest encouragement. The latency age child can be engaged in a discussion of the level of skill he or she wants to attain. A discussion can then follow as to how much practice will be necessary to attain the particular ambition held by the child. In this manner a child can feel they participated in a decision about how much to practice.

During latency allowances are probably introduced for the first time. My own sense is that it need not be more than a token sum during these years. The child should be permitted to spend it on whatever they want, assuming it is healthy and safe, although saving the allowance can be encouraged. I suggest that the allowance be connected up with the child being responsible for some token family chore at this age, for example, making their bed.

Parents often ask children to be responsible for a pet at this age. For example, they may be asked to walk a dog. My own belief is that this sort of responsibility, in some instances, may need to be postponed till they are pre-adolescents when they become more reliable. Pets can be very important in the life of a child. I am thinking of the companionship that a pet like a dog or cat can provide. For lonely children this can be invaluable. A child will have the opportunity to show affection and consideration towards another living creature and receive back affection and loyalty. In some instances they will need to be responsible for providing food, water, and exercise for their pet. If done well, I think it can only enhance a sense of competency. Of course, if the child seems to not have an inclination for a pet, the added responsibilities that parents may put on their child's shoulders will only feel like a burden and any positive outcome for the child will be diminished.

The attitudes of each gender towards one another differ during the latency years. Boys demean girls and exclude them. Some girls long to be included and comprise a group of girls we call "tomboys." These girls wish to participate in the more physical activities of boys and in play involving "masculine" themes, e.g., pretend warfare. Such girls often decry girlish clothes and play with dolls, but some tomboys do not and engage in both boyish and girlish activities. Also, even staunch tomboys often become feminine in late adolescence or early adulthood. Boys and girls that like each other will chase each other during school recess. If confronted by the other or someone else about whether or not they like the child they are chasing, the answer will be 'No." Sometimes they will go a step further and say they "hate" the child they are chasing. If the truth is known the child is convinced teasing will result.

Boys often have fewer friends than girls. Boys can have a chum with whom they are very close. When boys enter latency, they often have a foray back into the pre-oedipal days, so that oral and anal themes are never far away. How brief the foray is depends on the strength of pre-latency fixations. Recall, fixations are vulnerable earlier points in a person's developmental history. Boys may identify with mother to fend off her enveloping embrace that they regressively long for but are scared of, causing them to become anxious. The defense of identification backfires and the bisexual implications scare them. Closeness with boys can follow and is partly an evasive "homosexual" defense. This defense allows them not to invest in a wish for a baby or for breasts but instead to focus on masculine activities with a male friend. At times of transitions, when there is a tendency for regression to pre-oedipal closeness with mother, boys will defend against giving in to these wishes by reaching out to their own gender. It is "homosexual" **descriptively** only because of the sameness of gender. We will see it again during the transitions from latency to preadolescence, and from preadolescence to early adolescence. Girls generally have more successfully left behind the pre-oedipal connections to mother when they enter Latency. For some girls this may be because of their disappointment with her or their Oedipal rivalry with her. It is also more acceptable for girls to identify with mother than it is for boys to do so. Boys, on the other hand, have never really "let go" of mother. She is the primordial model for the future woman they will choose to have as a partner.

Presumably, in earliest infancy there existed a "unity" between mother and child. We theorize that this unity was a "blissful" union between infant and mother. This is speculative insofar as we cannot ask the infant to articulate their feelings. Mothers, however, will confirm how they felt as "one" with their fetus during pregnancy. We observe at various times in development during transitions, especially, regressive tendencies to re-establish pre-oedipal ties to mother. At the same time, there are signs of fear in the child of engulfment by the mother. Some have speculated there is an unconscious wish in the minds of children and mothers to re-establish the "unity" that once existed, to regain an undifferentiated state. If this is so, it is an ambivalent wish insofar as children also seem to have an inborn inclination to separate and be autonomous individuals, which mothers also support. Perhaps, the wish is gratified symbolically in the creative arts?

Girls form cliques and they are very exclusive. A lot of mean spiritedness towards outsiders can be expressed. If you are an outsider and it is important to be part of the group, this exclusion can be very painful. While boys are more outwardly aggressive and destructive, such backbiting by girls can be very hurtful. Some girls may feign illness in order to miss school when they are in the midst of these ostracisms. Identifications are endemic and are based on envy rather than on emulation. Despite the interpersonal drama, lifelong friendships among girls are capable. For some adult women, small groups of women can revive the schoolyard dynamics of their childhood. For both genders, heroes come to be important. For girls it is often media celebrities such as rock musical stars. While for boys this is also true, sport celebrities can be heroes. Parents can have a difficult time with their child's selection of a hero insofar as they often cannot see anything redeeming in the choice. As kids get older, choices will be based more on emulation than on envy.

Mid-latency would be the earliest I would consider sending a child off to sleep-away camp, perhaps for a week's duration, during the summer. I think pre-adolescents can handle such separations with greater ease and for longer durations. The experience can be very worthwhile in several ways. Lifetime recreational skills can be mastered, lifetime friendships can be fostered, and an increased sense of competency is possible. I would not, however, insist that children go to camp if they were strongly opposed to it. They must be ready for the experience.

In these contemporary times, mention should be paid to computers and other technology that will start to grab the focus of children beginning in late Latency. It once was not acceptable to be known as a "geek." This label once was an exclusive insult directed at technology-interested boys. Now to be called a "geek" or a "techie" is an honorarium directed at both sexes. Computers, cell phones, handheld Internet gadgets, i-pods, etc., are all part of the scene of children, particularly pre-adolescents and adolescents, but also among many latency age children. I am not sure what impact this has on intimacy. If you always are in touch with friends via cell phone, either talking or texting, does this increase intimacy or is it superficial? Does texting diminish face-to-face communication? Some older children stay up late on a school night in order to text and are tired the next morning. If you are listening to music on your i-pod and never make eye contact with passing people do you feel isolated or involved?

I do not think use of this technology has been around long enough to understand if it has an impact on the mind and on social relationships and what the quality of the impact is. I am concerned about children being allowed to play mindless interactive violent games on a handheld device, despite the fact that ratings should alert parents to the content. Some children spend an inordinate amount of time gaming. While there is not strong evidence that such violent games cause violent behavior, my concern is that children who are "gamers" live in a virtual reality rather than engage in the real world. Will this affect their awareness of social reality? Do adolescents lose sight of their physical limitations when in a cyberspace game they may take on new virtual identities (avatars) wherein they are omnipotent and where their virtual bodies have no physical limitations? Does this delay coming to terms with their changing pubertal physical bodies?

You can see we have more questions than answers at this point. The only thing of value I can intuit is that engaging such video games results in good eye-thumb coordination, and I would discourage use of such programs.

In this age of the Internet, parents can help their older latency age children understand about responsible and safe use of emailing, instant messaging, downloading cell phone digital photos (e.g., "sexting," wherein one sends provocative photos of oneself), engaging in Internet chat rooms, and web sites like My Space, Facebook, and YouTube. They need to understand the responsible use of free speech and to be wary of predators.

Parenting latency age children can be very fulfilling for both parent and child. It is a time when a child will still want to spend time with a parent doing activities. The activities chosen can include interests of the parent. Younger children may insist on fantasy play, an activity some adults may not be interested in. But the latency child is more interested in the world and learning about it. Parents can have their child accompany them to a sporting event, or coach a team that a child plays on. A child can sit through a concert or join in a trip to a museum for an extended time period, unlike a younger child whose interest likely will soon wane. Card games and board games will hold interest for a latency child. More complicated games like chess can be introduced. Family vacation options will broaden beyond Disneyland type venues.

Some fathers of latency age boys will have to come to terms with the fact that their son is not athletically inclined. Worse yet, the boy may be physically awkward and uncoordinated. For some fathers this will be difficult, especially for those who value athletics. More than whether or not you can throw and catch a football can define masculinity. I am sure there are parallels with mothers and daughters. The important thing is that our children fulfill their own unique potentialities and derive pleasure, satisfaction, and competence doing so.

Latency age children will be paying close attention to how their parents deal with other people. Are they polite or impolite, generous or stingy, respectful or disrespectful, civil or bossy, etc? They will notice if parents "walk the talk." Does their parent demand that they say "Please," but rarely does so him or herself when asking something of another person? Insofar as a child's conscience is a force to be reckoned with, they will use it against their parents as well. It is also an opportunity to further help them establish a conscience that has a sizeable reasonable component. If a parent acts reasonably with their children, they will likely be so with themselves and others too. The ability of a parent to apologize will go a long ways and helps their child to do similarly too. Parents best model thinking that is rational, reasonable, inquisitive, creative, and decisive. Parents likely have encouraged their children to "use" their "words" and parents need to as well to model that you can express feelings in a regulated and controlled manner.

A latency age child may be interested in what a parent does at their "work." A parent can talk about it and, if practical, even show their workplace to a son or daughter. It is beneficial for them see a parent who is competent and respected by others.

Interest in a child's schooling will strengthen their interest. If parents take the time to meet with a child's teachers and, if practical, become a room parent or volunteer for school trips, this can be very supportive to their child. Assistance given for school projects like a science fair can provide them with a model of thoughtfulness and perseverance. A parent best try not to be a model for procrastination. This trait if adopted by a child is difficult to be rid of and will be very burdensome throughout life. Being a "workaholic" also is not a trait to be admired.   Parents can hope that their child will emulate a reasonable work ethic, as well as a capacity to have fun.

Chapter 10
Divorce: Helping Children Cope

Divorce is a very difficult time for all family members. This is an understatement. It's often an upheaval because of a change in living arrangements and often it involves changes in life style because of economic considerations. As we have said earlier, children thrive on routine and divorce involves multiple changes. As much as sensitive parents try to insulate their child from witnessing spousal arguments, when parents are feeling estranged from each other, children also will not witness demonstrations of affection and cooperative behavior between these parents.

Should parents remain in an unhappy marriage because of children? The child will still witness the lack of love and intimacy between parents that remain married so the possible benefits of avoiding disruption may be cancelled out. Assuming the couple has made a genuine attempt to improve the marriage but failed, it seems to me divorce allows for the possibility of each parent eventually finding a better life and becoming a more happy and involved parent. Of course, a parent will need to deal empathically with the repercussions of the divorce on a child. In families with multiple children, each child's different reaction to the divorce needs to be attended to. Parents involved in a divorce often are preoccupied with their own unhappiness, or if they have been divorced for a while, parents may feel lonely and preoccupied with changing this for him or her. As a consequence, children can be neglected, especially if a downward economic situation causes a mother to return to work outside the home.

Children, especially young ones, are very egocentric or self-centered in their thinking. There is also the magical thinking that colors their immature cognitive processing. The consequence of this is to blame oneself for the divorce. If the parents have bickered because of differences in child rearing beliefs, children will feel responsible for parental arguments. They will deduce that their birth was the beginning of such arguments and caused their parents not to love each other anymore. Or a child will think that if he or she were a more satisfying child the parent would have decided not to leave the marriage. If children harbor a wish, albeit maybe not even a conscious one, for parents to separate, the boy or girl may feel responsible. Struggling with such a wish is a common dynamic during the Oedipal years. It may be buried deep within the recesses of the mind, but, nevertheless, if the wish comes true the child likely will experience guilt. Some children will take on a mediator role. They may enact this more openly with friends who are in dispute, and more subtly with parents who argue. This sense of needing to mediate or to protect a parent perceived to be the weaker of the two parents is very burdensome to a child. After all, a child needs to feel that the adults in their life are protecting he or she and not vice versa. After a divorce of their parents, a child may become very watchful of the mood of a parent and may feel that it is their responsibility to cheer them up if they appear depressed lest they may leave and abandon the child.

Parents can help mitigate but not eradicate such self-blame by talking to their children about the reasons for the divorce, emphasizing that the child is not to blame. Some reasons for a decision to separate might have to be omitted until the child is older and asks for more details and can understand better. I am thinking here of a reason such as infidelity. It is important that parents do not blame the spouse for the divorce, or "bad-mouth" the spouse in front of the child. Remember that the child has deep ties to each parent and blame can lead to hatred and estrangement. When divorced spouses are very angry with each other this may be difficult not to do, but it is worth it for the child's sake. Sometimes ex-spouses take out their anger for the other in ways that directly or indirectly hurt the child. For example, holding out on financial obligations until the last minute, not arriving for visitation on schedule so the ex-spouse is inconvenienced, etc., will hurt the child too. Children hope that their divorced parents will reconcile. They may also feel responsible for reconciling their parents. An unconscious belief in their own omnipotence stimulates such efforts.

Custody decisions need to be made with the best interests of the child given priority. Remember that young children like stability, and the living arrangements should accommodate this. If so, children should not be shuttled back and forth between the divorced parents so that each has "equal time" with the children. It is thoughtful if living arrangements are concentrated in one household and visitation occurs within the other. An ideal arrangement is for the family house or apartment to be maintained and the parents shuttle in and out. This way the family space is not disrupted and children, especially young ones, are least unsettled. Of course, for such an arrangement, spouses must feel amiable towards each other and also practical considerations likely will make such an ideal arrangement impractical. When choosing separate domiciles, preferably they are within close proximity to one another. For the latency age and older child, this will allow a walk or bicycle ride over to the other parent in a spontaneous way if there is a special need.

If a divorced parent is dating, this best occurs in a discreet way. What I mean is that it does not benefit the child to be introduced to and be involved with every person a parent is engaged with in a relationship. This is to be avoided because of the feelings of loss that could be engendered if a connection is established and the relationship ends. If there is a serious relationship that will endure and maybe become permanent then introductions and involvements will inevitably happen. Here a divorced parent benefits their child if they establish a working relationship with their ex-spouse's new partner. A divorced parent can indicate to their child that it is all right to establish a good relationship with father's or mother's new partner. A parent needs to let their child know this will not hurt the parent's feelings. If there is ill will the child will sense it and loyalty issues will ensue.

Perhaps a divorced parent remarries. The new partner may have children and may even be a primary custodial parent. These arrangements are known as blended families. Stepparents now enter the picture. This can be a difficult relationship for former spouses and the new spouse. This also can be difficult for the stepparent and stepchild. Each knows they are not the biological parent or child. Recall the brothers Grimm's mythic tale of Snow White illustrating the fury of an envious stepmother towards her beautiful stepdaughter. How much authority does the stepparent have and what compliance does the stepchild need to have with them? Each blended family will need to work on this and establish sensible and practical guidelines. I think it is sensible for the adults to acknowledge the difficulties and confusion that may beset their children and affirm the tie to the biological parent. With time and multiple empathic interchanges between stepparent and stepchild, a good relationship can develop, loving and growth promoting for each participant.

Likely, there is an inborn incest barrier between biological parent and child. In the case of a stepparent and stepchild this will be absent. The presence of such a barrier, regrettably, does not prevent incest or sexual abuse, nor will its absence necessarily cause sexual abuse. Even in intact families, issues of modesty and over stimulation remain and need to be on the radar screen, too, of blended families.

What if the blended family brings together children from each partner? They may be of similar ages and the same or different gender. Step-sibs need to be dealt with. In many instances this can be a fulfilling relationship for a lifetime. But for others it can be strained. There can be issues of favoritism of a stepparent towards their biological child, or perception of such on the part of a child about the stepparent. A stepparent needs to be aware of this and fairness be accepted as a goal. Strain can enter if a blended family has two adolescents of similar age but opposite gender. Sexual attraction can be an underlying determinant of a tense relationship between the two. Friction and bickering may be defensively employed as a way of keeping distance between each other. Presumably, once each establishes a heterosexual relationship outside the family, the tension will remit. But until it does remit, the biological parent and stepparent can offer to be mediators. In serious cases, one adolescent can temporarily live with the other biological parent, or if this is not possible or practical, professional help may need to be obtained.

Chapter 11

Sex Education, Media Exposure, and After-School Enrichment

Sex Education

From the above you have learned that young children are sexual to begin with, not in the usual adult sense, but that sexual (libidinal) pleasure is a feeling that they experience. Perhaps, you have come to this observation independently. The question probably has arisen in your mind as to what is the best age to provide sex education to a child and who should dispense it. Earlier, I pointed out that children create theories of their own about conception and birth based on limited personal experiences and bits of information they have gathered from different sources. For example, that conception is oral and based on eating, and birth is anal and based on elimination.

My own belief is that parents, preferably the parent of the same gender as the child, should provide sex education. I want to distinguish between answering a child's questions about sex which can occur at different ages and parents taking the initiative, raising the topic, and providing information if their child avoids it. I suggest that the mother talk with her daughter and the father with his son because this likely will be experienced by the child as less seductive. I am thinking of a parent taking the initiative when the child is preadolescent. The facts of procreation and reassurance about masturbation can be imparted and comprehended.

At an earlier age, children will ask questions indicating curiosity about conception and birth. Most likely, both a boy and girl will ask their mother but fathers get asked too. The question may not be direct, such as, "How do babies get made?" Instead, you might have to infer it from observations the child makes about a pregnant woman or queries about storks bringing babies and dropping them off at homes. Some children know of pets that have had babies and they ask questions about this. Some latency children might start using the "f word" as an indirect way of expressing sexual curiosity. Many parents have qualms about explaining how a sperm gets into a mommy to fertilize an egg. I advise to answer a question first by asking a child to tell you what they believe. If the child has a misconception then it should be corrected with the facts. Information should not be provided beyond the answer called for by the child's question. In other words, let the child process or digest what they have been told. To give more information will only over load the child's mind. It may take months before the child asks another question. Children need to be allowed to go at their own pace.

This is why I do not think sex education should be taught to young children in schools where individual differences cannot be accommodated as they can in a family. However, human reproduction should be in the curriculum for adolescents along with information about birth control, including abstinence, in my view. If there is an objection to this on religious grounds, then these children can be absent and instead abstinence can be discussed by the parents or by a religious institution. Many parents prefer euphemisms to the correct scientific terms for anatomical parts. This is because of the adult's own discomfort talking openly about sex. I discourage this because it contributes a quality of shame to the topic. A penis is a "penis" and not a "wee wee." A vagina is a "vagina" and not a "hole" or "private."

I do believe young children need to be educated, without alarming them, to be wary of strangers who invite them to accompany them with bribes of candy or other enticements. Also young children can be told that their bodies are private and unless they have the permission of a parent or parent surrogate, or one of these people are present, they should refuse to allow an adult or older child to touch parts of their body covered by underwear.

Media Exposure

Media exposure has become an issue particularly since 9/11. Many children were exposed to the news as countless parents listened to it in cars and on television, too shocked to turn it off when their children were within earshot or watching the television along with them. They heard things or saw images that were scary and watched as their parents were horrified, conveying shock, fear, and helplessness, all of which exacerbated their own fright. If adults cannot comprehend terror they cannot expect that a three, five, or eight year old can do so. This is an instance where censorship is meaningful. Young children of fearful and anxious mothers are more fearful and anxious than children whose mothers are not so.

Parents need to be prepared, however, to help young children process thoughts and feelings so they can begin to comprehend events such as terrorism or naturally occurring disasters like earthquakes. Even if a parent exercises caution in one's own home as to what children are exposed to by the media or conversation, other households may not and likely a child will hear about or see some images pertaining to a terrorist act or natural disaster. Words can be used that children can understand and can be reassured it is unlikely that where you live a natural disaster will occur, or if it might, tell them of the precautions being taken. Some children, even after processing the facts of a natural disaster, may continue to be preoccupied by such events or even show a fascination with them. In my experience natural disasters such as tornados are used, like a metaphor, for some children to communicate their worries, without conscious awareness, about losing control over some intense inner feelings, such as anger. This is their mind's way of trying to master (regulate) these feelings. By learning the facts about tornadoes and safety precautions regarding them, children process, albeit in a displaced way, thoughts accompanied with anxiety about imagined consequences of expressing uncontrollable impulses.

In general, it is a good idea not to use television as a baby-sitter, especially with young children. An adult alongside them can help them comprehend what they are viewing. Also, parents can take every opportunity to enjoy and have their child enjoy the interactive pleasures of a common experience. Of course, there will be many instances when a parent will need to be busy with a task, such as preparing the family dinner, and cannot be attentive to child-care. On such occasions, television can serve as a safe activity for a child. However, in some instances, a pre-selected DVD might be a better choice than a television show whose content a parent has no control over.

A related issue, is a child hearing about illnesses that parents of friends or relatives have been stricken by, or even peers. Concerns about dying and death may follow. The reality is that people get ill, sometimes fatally, and the older you are the greater the risk. This fact can be conveyed to concerned children. My own belief is that parents should not overwhelm children about the harsh aspects of reality but if they are exposed to them nor should a parent lie. Parents should always be allied with reality and not fantasy. This will help their child do the same and not feel betrayed by a parent. It also will encourage them to use parents as a resource about reality.

After-School Enrichment

Parents these days are very concerned about helping their children have a "step up" on their peers, rivals for a place at a prestigious college in the future. In the past twenty years, there has been a growth of after-school enrichment programs. Many of these are involving athletic skills such as soccer or hockey (which may even take place before school to insure ice rink availability), or talents in areas such as music, drama, or art. My belief is that when used judiciously, such activities make sense. They cater to a child's interests and strengths. The enhancement of skills and development of talent increases a child's self-esteem. I do not, however, think it increases a child's chances for acceptance at Harvard if enrollment in such activities is included on a resume. Thus, whether it is sensible or not to have a child participate has to do with the purpose of such involvement. Is it initiated by the child, agreed to, or coerced upon the child? There is value for a child to have leisure time to do whatever it is that he or she likes to do, even if its to daydream, climb a tree, play with the dog, etc. It may appear to some parents that there is little redeeming in these activities, but the child may disagree. Having fun is part of childhood, too.

Some older children want to use the computer or watch television after school. My own belief is that children need some kind of physical activity to inculcate a positive attitude about physical exercise. If a child dislikes team sports then there are non-competitive and/or solitary physical activities like bicycling, swimming, gymnastics, skate boarding, etc. I think there needs to be a limit on how many hours a day television is watched. Also, selection of programs may need parental oversight. The same goes for video games. I do not recommend that I-phones and other such devices be used as toys for toddlers. Children at this age learn best by physically engaging their environments. Parents engaging verbally promote language skills with their children. The use of a computer by older children is more complicated. Assuming the use is more than to play games or to go to inappropriate Internet sites, becoming skillful with a computer has redeeming value given its central role in our modern world. This, however, does not require endless hours looking at a computer screen.

Reading good children's literature is a very worthwhile activity for after-school. It will increase children's vocabularies, stimulate their imaginations, contribute positively to their narrative skills, both spoken and written, and increase their knowledge of the world. A child might gravitate towards comic books. Some of these are of a high caliber, being well drawn and having a worthwhile message. More importantly, the child will be reading.

Chapter 12
Sexual Abuse

There seems to be an "epidemic" of sexual abuse reports in the media. I do not think we really know if the incidence is greater than years ago. In any case, it is always alarming to hear reports about this. My definition of sexual abuse is probably narrower in some respects and broader in others, than what is commonly talked about. Sexual abuse to me is when an adult or older child knowingly exploits a younger child for purposes of gaining their own sexual pleasure. To satisfy this definition, it does not require physical contact, like penetration, fellatio, cunnilingus, or touching of genitals. Such actions are clearly sexually abusive. It could, however, be repeated immodesty about nakedness or exposure to pornography. Or it could be parents never taking precautions, keeping the bedroom door open or unlocked, so the child is repeatedly exposed to parents engaged in sexual acts. Some parents allow the child to be present in the bathroom as they bathe or in the dressing room as they get dressed to go out. This is unnecessary and too stimulating. All of the above are seductive, sometimes intentionally. It is misguided to think that exposing children to nakedness and immodesty will allow them to be less "neurotic" about their bodies. What is the child to do with the excitement? Often they "act up."

I include in my definition of sexual abuse a disparity in ages between the doer and recipient. This is important because young children under the age of six express sexual curiosity by exposing their bodies to one another or by playing "doctor." Usually, they are of similar age. This is voluntary and does not have deleterious effects. It might if the instigator was an older cousin, like an adolescent, or a baby sitter. The differences in the size and appearance of the genital will likely be frightening to the much younger observer.

Children who are sexually abused often repeat the abuse with other children. Parents may not know directly that their child has been abused. Children tend to be ashamed or guilty and are scared of punishment and keep the experience(s) secret. Sometimes they may feel guilty because at some level they may be aware of their own sexual wishes, or, possibly, of pleasure they experienced. I state this not to blame the victim but to underscore the self-blame of victims. This is especially so if incest is involved. The guilt is exacerbated because of continual contact with the abuser, someone whom they love.

If a child becomes acutely anxious, a gentle inquiry about whether he or she have been frightened recently by something might encourage them to volunteer events they are ashamed of or frightened about. I am not encouraging asking direct or leading questions. There have been reports of claims of sexual abuse that are really reports of sexual fantasies. Sometimes, adults, mainly fathers, have been falsely accused of abusing their own children. Professional help may be required for a child to disclose the abuse and later to process the sequela. When the abuse has not been a single event (shock trauma) but rather a cumulative trauma, the etiological significance of the incidents in the total dynamic picture of the child may be harder to specify.

Chapter 13
Pre-adolescence

The hormonal changes associated with puberty begin to express themselves usually around age ten or eleven for girls and usually a year later for boys. Girls may start to have some acne, have some underarm odor, sprout buds on their chests, and get a little taller. Menses usually is a couple of years away. Girls seem to be menstruating earlier these days, perhaps as a result of nutritional factors or additives put into foods. Boys follow in maturing. They may have an initial lowering of their voices. Facial hair will usually not appear until further into puberty. Penile emissions are usually a couple of years in the future. We call this the pre-adolescent phase of development.

This can be a difficult time for children. Girls may be proud of their beginning breast development. They may anticipate its arrival by purchasing bras before they really need them. Many, however, try to hide it by slouching when they stand. It is not uncommon to see girls with rounded shoulders during these years and into early adolescence. Some find it difficult to be the only one in their group of friends who has begun breast development. Boys can be embarrassed by voice changes that are erratic.

For both genders, but especially for boys, the beginning of pre-adolescence can be stressful enough that a regression in drives may appear. Recall, the focus on their bodies just before entering the latency years was on the genitals. During these pre-adolescent years there can be a re-awakening of even earlier types of drives. There is an indiscriminant arousal of excitement. Boys can become very crude in an anal way. Anal sounds are joked about, and a fart can reduce a group of boys to laugh uncontrollably. Orality may demonstrate itself in excessive drinking of soda pop or eating of sweets, a feature for either gender.

Girls seem more resistant to this regression around the onset of the pre-adolescent years. This seems so, as mentioned earlier, because they appear to have more completely repressed earlier types of wishes prior to entering the Oedipal drama. They shifted their attention to father from their mothers. Hence, early type wishes that center on mother may be less available to girls when pre-adolescence begins. When I speak of the diminished ties girls have for mothers I am not referring to overt behavior. Rather, being **like** mother (identification) predominates over a focus on mother for pleasure seeking (object desire). Boys, on the other hand, as mentioned earlier, have not reduced ties to their mothers but have only changed their aims. Within their minds, or intrapsychically, investing mother as an object of desire, especially genital desire, diminishes for girls. For a minority of girls the closeness stemming from identification makes it difficult to separate from mother. Most girls as women, however, are able to satisfy residual feelings for closeness originating in their tie to mother via mature relationships with female friends. They can be close and sharing while maintaining separateness and autonomy.

Girls and boys differ as to how they regard each other. Boys seem scared of girls, who are usually more mature, both physically and psychically. They defend against this fear by demeaning girls. This fear of girls includes mother. Boys are drawn to mother because of the reawakening of passive longings. These longings, however, also scare them. Boys can become afraid of being enveloped by their mothers. There may be a re-emergence of the unconscious wish for a baby. Bi-sexual conflict intensifies castration anxiety. They identify with the active mother, the doer, (in their minds, the so-called "phallic woman"), as a defense against their own passive wishes. To deal with all of these dynamics, boys immerse themselves with a male peer. This is a sort of evasive homosexual period that is transitory. This dynamic for the pre-adolescent boys is reminiscent of the same unconscious dynamic experienced during the transition from the Oedipal phase into Latency. (As mentioned earlier, the use of the term "homosexual" if used **prior** to puberty is used descriptively only. It is only after puberty that sexual orientation is decided upon.)

Girls, on the other hand, run in packs and boys view them like Amazons. The girls are full of secrets and shifting alliances. One day a particular girl may be part of the group but the next day she is excluded. For a few girls there can be a pseudo-heterosexuality that might appear on the surface to be the real thing, but underneath the aim is to overcome fear of and resist a resurgence of earlier modes of drive expression involving mother. Girls can be interested in smutty topics but too direct sexual interests are not yet part of the culture of this age group. They become ardent fans of female pop singers and some may profess crushes on these pop stars or even on a male teenage pop singer. Girls particularly want to be like every one else in their group. The pre-adolescent girl who does not wear braces on her teeth may feel like an "outsider."

Some boys may become bullies to other boys. It may become physical. The motives vary but what may be in common for bullies of either gender is attributing their own hated personality or physical features to their intended victims. Bullying behavior discloses unconscious feelings of inferiority. Perhaps, too, it may be an externalization of unconscious sado-masochistic wishes upon the chosen victim? Girls can be particularly mean to other girls during this stage. Bullying from girls takes the form of excluding and verbally denigrating another girl. Intervention needs to help the injured party not to feel victimized and the perpetrator to feel more empathy for the intended victim. Peer confrontation of bullies under adult guidance has proven to be useful.

Parents can find this a particularly trying time. The beginning defiance of the pre-adolescent can be disturbing. What happened to the cherubic little boy or girl? The child's interest in a popular pop star whose lyrics are suggestive becomes an issue. A change in tastes regarding clothes based on older adolescent trends is unsettling to parents. For girls, an initial interest in the opposite sex can cause parents to become nervous. The pubertal bodily changes, not yet in noticeable bloom, can begin to be very disturbing to some parents. Fathers begin to feel uncomfortable having their daughters squirming on their laps. The immodesty of children can be difficult, especially when they are beginning to show pubertal changes. More about that when we discuss adolescence proper.

This is a good opportunity for fathers to do more things with their sons and mothers with their daughters. Of course, doing things with a child of the opposite sex is not so easy at this age because of gender-specific interests of some. Children of this age seem to feel embarrassment to be seen in the company of a parent by their peers. Parents can participate with their children in interests that the child enjoys in non-public venues.

Pre-adolescence is a good time for parents to consider the introduction of serious responsibilities to be assigned to their child. What I have in mine are such household chores as expecting your child to do his or her own laundry, to be responsible for tasks such as help in preparing family meals by setting the table, or cleaning up, or in some cooking, or in maintenance tasks such as cutting the grass, taking out the garbage, shoveling snow, etc. If there is a family pet, tasks such as feeding them and walking the dog or changing the cat's litter box are all reasonable requests. The pre-adolescent is old enough to be reliable and competent in carrying out these tasks. Additionally, lifelong skills will be learned and self-esteem in feeling competent and responsible will be enhanced. Allowance can be connected to such family services. Learning about saving money and budgeting it is also a skill that can be inculcated. When children get older they can be given a lump sum of money and be asked to budget it for the purchase of clothes.

Chapter 14
Early Adolescence

Do you recall your entry into adolescence? It is not as if one day you were pre-adolescent and the next day you were a full-fledged adolescent. Unless we substitute pre-teen and teenage as the criteria for the division, then, you became a teenager on your thirteen birthday. Of course, there are the pubertal changes that herald entry into adolescence. Recall that during pre-adolescence puberty begins in a less noticeable manner. The onset of puberty proper or sexual maturity that is more noticeable varies from individual to individual. For girls sexual maturity usually begins earlier than for boys. For many girls maturation could be achieved by age twelve or thirteen, and for boys at age thirteen or fourteen. There are many healthy adolescents who mature later. There are rare instances of precocious sexual maturity, mostly in girls, as early as mid-latency. Precocious puberty of this sort is a medical glandular abnormality. But adolescence, mainly, is a psychological concept. It kind of coincides with entry into high school. Some cultures provide initiation rites of one sort or another to mark the entry into adolescence. Adolescence predominantly has to do with a change in the way you see yourself and others and how you relate to them. For girls physical changes with maturation are more noticeable. Such changes can be a source of shame or pride.

Let us imagine what an early adolescent boy or girl might be thinking (expurgated). Our imaginary girl may be thinking the following: "I'm starting to menstruate and need to be concerned about personal hygiene because of these 'periods.' Sometimes I want to scream! I don't want dad to know I have got my first period but I know mom will tell him and I'll feel embarrassed in his company. How do I master putting in a tampon? 'Bad hair days' can ruin my day. Why am I so vain? Thank heaven for jeans. I can always wear them. The more faded the better. Why was it stylish for them to be torn last year but not this year? And they are so expensive. I need to have the designer jeans like the other girls. They are so tight, I can hardly get into them, but it's worth the struggle to get the boys to notice. My first high heels! How do you walk in these? The boys seem to like them so I'll suffer. Ugh! This bra is so uncomfortable but it makes me look bigger than I am and I see the boys noticing me more, so I'll put up with it. Will my breasts get bigger this year?"

Our imaginary boy is thinking: "I worry about nocturnal emissions that will need to be hidden from my mom. Even worse are the spontaneous erections when I'm in class. What will I do if the teacher asks me to go up to the black board? I really want to become "buff" and feel strong so that both girls and guys will notice. I don't know why I wear my pants so low that it looks as if they are ready to fall off, but I want to look cool. Which way are baseball hats to be turned this year? Shoes are a whole other matter. My parents tell me that I need to wear leather shoes if I get dressed up and wear a suit but I don't have any."

Both genders also likely are having thoughts about the other gender's body. A girl may notice a cute boy and embarrassedly imagine him as a boyfriend but notice, with dismay, he is a head shorter than she. A boy, with titillation, may notice the same girl looking furtively at him but lament privately that the other kids will tease him that he only comes up to her chin.

Both genders share some common thoughts: " 'Zits' or acne makes me not want to be seen. Mom tells me repetitively to wash my face and to exercise self-control about not squeezing pimples. My appetite can be ravenous, especially after I get home from school. I can eat a whole box of doughnuts or a whole loaf of bread. I worry constantly about gaining weight. I can sleep to noon on a weekend morning. I am always tired from going to sleep too late to get up before the sun does in order to get to school on time before the first bell in the morning. I need to take showers daily because if I don't the other kids might tease me about body odor. Before I could get away with not taking them unless my parents made a big deal about it. Will I get taller this year?"

Let us look for the "silver lining" for a moment. It is with the beginning of adolescence that the process of taking "ownership" of one's own body really begins. Adolescents will become increasingly responsible for personal hygiene, for dressing appropriately for the weather, for taking medicines, and even for eating properly. But do not expect this to happen abruptly. An adolescent still may go out on a cold winter's day wearing a tee shirt and shorts.

I know I am presenting a picture of a superficial person and adolescents are much more than that. There are many who are fervent about humanistic causes. I will speak more about that later. But concerns about appearance suddenly reach ascendancy. "I'm overweight and no boy will ever ask me on a date. I cannot stop eating." "I'm shorter than almost every girl in my class."

Regretfully, the adolescent girl who laments about her weight is not in touch with the underlying feelings about how food is a symbolic substitute for other things. She can be so self-conscious about being overweight she will be inconsolable. Another boy or girl is so shy, they feel so awkward around the opposite sex. In the privacy of their bedroom they can rhythmically and gracefully move their body to the music on their i-pod but it's impossible to do this in public. They rather not go to the party. To be popular is an ideal. The popular girls and boys are envied. Let me continue with my portrayal of the imagined private thoughts of my composite early adolescent girl or boy.

"School is so stressful. The adults all tell me that grades now count. I practically have to be a straight-A student to be able to get into the state university. Some how, I need to stand out from all the other students with straight-As to be noticed by any prestigious school. What 'good cause' should I volunteer for so I can put this on my college application? I cannot think that far ahead. I'm worried about the exam tomorrow or how to get up enough guts to talk to the girl (boy) sitting alongside me. I feel such intense feelings I sometimes even feel suicidal. Whom can I confide in? My parents won't understand, they're too old. I need a best friend more than anything else in the world. Maybe my dog will do in the meantime. I know, I'll eat a doughnut or get high and it won't matter."

Of course, the above reveries are not those of all early adolescents, but regretfully, of too many to dismiss them as of little concern. It is a tough time and we do not pay enough attention to this age period. Educators in the USA have tried to come up with the most suitable arrangement for learning. There used to be "junior high schools" which 7th, 8th, and 9th graders attended. It was believed the 9th graders were too immature to be with older high school students. Now, instead there are "middle schools" where 6th, 7th and 8th graders attend. It was felt that the 9th graders were too mature for the 7th and 8th graders so they were grouped once again with older students. You can see there is not a simple solution!

Unlike the above composite adolescent, there are many early adolescents who are enthusiastic about the changes they are ongoing. They are engaged in school and extra-curricular activities like sports and with family. They are pleased with their growth spurt and proud of their maturing bodies. A mother has told the girl who is menstruating for the first time that it is a sign of health and progress and a symbol of her femininity and generative powers. A boy who has a mother that admires his newfound strength and stature without being seductive and a father who welcomes his son almost beating him at tennis allows a boy to feel comfortable with his burgeoning masculinity. It helps a pubescent girl if her mother is comfortable with her own mature body and her femininity. After all, her mother is a model to emulate.

Some women have problems with menstrual cycles, whether the problems are caused by psychological or biological factors. If they get pre-menstrual symptoms and are temporarily "put out of commission," their daughters may take this as a model. There is a saying, "The acorn doesn't fall far from the oak tree," which, regrettably, is true about children and parents. The former identify with the latter, which is a good thing if we're speaking of desirable traits, but an unfortunate thing if it involves traits that the child swore never to adopt. If a father compensates for a strong identification with his own mother by being demeaning of passive men and acts excessively macho, pity his early adolescent son who is not interested in "manly" activities. What if this son has to "do" the father "one better" and becomes a schoolyard bully and misogynous?

What is the most important psychological task of the adolescence phase of development? I would say that it is to find a non-incestuous person to love. The primary love interests of children are their parents. They have to accept the premise, intrapsychically, that they eventually will need to find a person to love sexually that minimally links up with a parent. I do not mean to imply that this is accomplished as a decision via conscious problem solving. Instead, an unconscious struggle goes on within the psyche (mind) that can cause much internal and external conflict. If this is not accomplished, more than less, by the end of adolescence, the adolescent likely will experience conflict with their future partner. We call this achievement object removal. We are wrong to think that the Oedipal Complex is ever fully eradicated. It's effects wax and wane throughout our lives.

A correlated task of adolescence is what is called the second separation-individuation. In early childhood, it was an accomplishment to be able to separate from the physical mother (first separation-individuation). Once accomplished, the child is able to begin to function autonomously with peers and other adults. This was achieved by means of consolidating the image internally of mother (object constancy), as discussed earlier. Now, the adolescent must be able to disengage from the internal representation of the childhood parent(s). Actually, transformation is more accurate than disengagement. This achievement and object removal are interwoven processes.

Another important task of adolescence is for the adolescent to come to terms with his or her maturing sexual body. The adolescent is now capable of conceiving a baby in reality, not just in fantasy. Accompanying their mature bodies are sexual urges towards other persons, usually of the opposite gender, but sometimes directed at someone of the same gender. Thus, the issue of sexual orientation is a correlated task of coming to terms with one's maturing body. I will speak more about sexual orientation in the chapter below dealing with homosexuality.

Corresponding to their child's separation-individuation efforts, parents, too, are undergoing developmental changes in parenthood. They, too, need to psychically allow their child to emancipate. The beginning of this process occurred earlier when their child was physically separating from them during their third year of life, and then again as the child moved into the latency years, weakening their Oedipal ties to them. Some parents find this change in the nature of their parenting to be difficult while some welcome the opportunities to have more leisure time to pursue interests. For those where the change is difficult they have trouble modifying their self-image as a parent defined mainly as attentive to a dependent child to that of being a parent to an independent and more self-reliant child.

A consequence of beginning the processes of object removal and the second separation-individuation is for the early adolescent to start to feel an inner emptiness or internal void, as well as feelings of loneliness. The adolescent is not consciously aware that this intrapsychic process is ongoing. Insofar as the internalized parental objects are the foundation for the conscience (the mental agency comprised of prohibitions and ideals), disengagement from parents weakens the adolescent's ability to exercise self-control over feelings and urges. Hence, a regulatory agency of the mind is put sufficiently out of commission. The ego, the executive part of the mind, loses an ally, or is left with a weakened ally. This, however, allows for the adolescent gradually to revise his or her superego so that it can become more mature in its expectations insofar as it no longer needs to be based solely upon early parental introjects. Hence, early on in the process of secondary separation-individuation and object removal, adolescents have a proclivity to act out, to disregard prohibitions. The peer group's moral code is adopted. Hopefully, the peer group is not a delinquent one. Friends feel very important to adolescents, even more so than parents. Adolescents are very susceptible to peer pressure. Have you had to deal with an adolescent on vacation away from his friend(s)? They always welcome inviting a friend along. With cell phones these days they are always in touch with their friends. Later, we will discuss the means to which some adolescents go to attempt to fill the inner void felt after they disengage from their primary objects (parents).

Acting-out, or engaging in un-regulated behaviors, can be reduced if an early adolescent has a close friend. The friend becomes a confidant. The chum chosen is based on an ideal self-image and the friendship thereby "absorbs" feelings about the self (narcissistic feelings) and is a homosexual choice insofar as one chooses someone like oneself. Hence, it is not based on libidinal desire but on narcissism. The earlier homosexual stance of preadolescence was a defensive one to ward off passive identificatory wishes directed at mother. During early adolescence, it is based on an idealized view of oneself, the person the adolescent wishes to be like. This, too, is usually temporary for the boy who usually is ashamed and uncomfortable with his femininity and bisexuality.

Friendships are also important for the early adolescent girl. Without one she can become depressed. The "crush," beginning in pre-adolescence, comes more into play, either towards another girl or a boy. This eroticized relationship also is based, like the boy, on an ideal self-image. Girls find it more acceptable to claim their masculinity than do boys to claim their femininity. In the "crush" she can play the male role if the friend is a girl, or insist on equality if the friend is a boy. For most girls, this bisexual position will be abandoned during later adolescence for a heterosexual one. There will be proud acceptance of her femaleness and her whole body's femininity. For a minority of girls there will occur sexual acting out, sometimes in a promiscuous way. This is defensive against puberty's re-awakening of early needs involving mother. The girl will mal-adaptively, without conscious awareness, seek to satisfy such needs through sex. It is the unconscious wish to be held, as the girl once was by mother, and not to be penetrated sexually, which is sought.

An interest that is very important to many early adolescents is music. Some adolescents are almost preoccupied with music. You can see them always listening to their i-pods. A few may have an interest in learning how to play a musical instrument such as a guitar. The music allegiance of each generation differs as to genre or to group or individual pop stars. One generation may feel unable to relate to the next generation's musical interest. It may be that this gulf of musical appreciation, and popular culture in general, helps to facilitate the separation of the adolescent from the older generation and gives them solidarity with their own generation at a time when they feel a reduction of affiliation with parents.

Sports are another activity that many adolescents gravitate towards. Parents can be supportive of their adolescent's interests. Since the passage of Title IX more girls in the States are also participating in sports. Many adolescents are aware of their bodies' new strength and agility. Young adolescents enjoy the competitiveness and exhibitionism of being a talented athlete. Some are too conflicted about both to participate in sports. Some girls may seriously engage in dance during these years. For others, the exhibitionism is too conflicted and cannot be overcome. A few girls may be able to participate in equestrian activities. Athletic or dance talents can be a source of positive self-esteem for many adolescents. Involvement in team sports, allowing for camaraderie and physical contact, is an opportunity for boys and girls to sublimate homoerotic feelings.

Parents during this phase of early adolescence need to make themselves available. As mentioned earlier, when we discussed pre-adolescence, fathers and mothers can, respectively, help their sons and daughters by participating in enjoyable activities together. With opposite sex children, it might be easier for the child if a friend is invited to join. "Togetherness" might feel impossible for parents because of the defiant attitude of their child. Its worth the effort for parents to overcome their self-protectiveness against rebuffs. A parent should never be seductive. To be so is always destructive but it is particularly so during a child's adolescence. Parents need to remember, it is the behavior that is abhorred, not the child, whom is loved. This needs to be made clear to children.

During this age period, it is important that parents maintain their stance about limits and reasonable consequences when there is disobedience about them. Parents need to try to live up to their own standards that they hold their children to. Otherwise, an adolescent will show up a parent's hypocrisy and it will be very disillusioning for them and encourage further estrangement from adult values. Parents best try to remain the adult in the family. If a parent tries to act like an adolescent with the aim of bonding this is misguided. Adolescents need adult parents, as much as they say they disregard them. At some level, if a parent objects to their outlandish behavior, he or she will notice that you care and it will pay dividends later on. So, parents are advised, for example, not to smoke pot with their children or accompany them to movies that are aimed for the adolescent market. At least, do not sit with your adolescent and his or her friends.

An issue that invariably arises during a child's early adolescence in connection with entry into high school is whether or not parents should remind their child to study and/or do homework. Parents are very aware of how competitive it is to gain entry into good colleges. I think that by this age most children also are aware of the need to study and to do one's homework. They are at an age when self-motivation and self-responsibility ordinarily is internalized. There are some children who may have serious impairments in concentration and organization that may need more parental supervision. Parents can make clear their expectations regarding priorities but children need to establish their own priorities. Inherent in making poor choices will be natural consequences, e.g., an inferior grade. The last thing a parent needs to do is to get embroiled in a power struggle with their early adolescent. The switch from middle school to high school will take some period of adjustment. Parents can enter a dialogue with their youngster as to how they can be of assistance. If rejected they can let their child know the invitation is still there. They can agree with the child that they will not micromanage, as it seems to have negative effects. I would encourage parents to help their child organize a plan to balance schoolwork and leisure activities. Parents and children can agree to revisit the issue if expected results are not met.

Chapter 15
Middle Adolescence

What was begun in early adolescence progresses further during middle adolescence. By its completion most adolescents have successfully transformed the ties to their parents and they have made the switch to a heterosexual choice that is not intimately linked to the parent of the opposite sex, a non-incestuous choice. As a result of this internal process, many adolescents are feeling a sense of loss, and, simultaneously, for those who are in a relationship, a feeling of "being in love." Sexual orientation is settled for most adolescents. By sexual orientation we mean adoption of homosexuality or heterosexuality as the preferred choice of a partner. This is different from gender identity by which we mean acceptance of being male or female. This is firmly established by age three*. Gender role involves behavior that is masculine or feminine.

As mentioned above, the process of disattachment to the "infantile" objects (parents) results in feeling lonely and an inner feeling of emptiness that the adolescent tries to fill in different ways. We call such attempts restitutive. The adolescent cannot simply undo the ties without painful feelings akin to mourning. At an unconscious level, there are wishes to re-establish the infantile ties, but there is also resistance to this. Adolescents really need to transform the nature of their tie to infantile objects. Severing ties is not in any one's best interests, in most instances. Exceptions might be if a parent has been abusive or criminal. A new object must be acceptable to all of the mental agencies involved in the adolescent's mind. Adolescents seek to substitute the relationship with parents with identification, particularly to the parent of the same sex. Until this is successful, they will make transitory identifications with all sorts of people, some "good" and some "bad." The bad ones are troublesome because of the weakened

---

*Gender identity is less fixed, however, than psychoanalysis has believed given the current incidence of transgender issues.

status of their conscience. Identifications with unethical figures could encourage delinquency.

One way that restitution is attempted is to shift the emotional investment withdrawn from the parents and re-distribute it upon oneself. This often is temporary until a new object has been invested in. We call this self-investment narcissistic. A result is that many adolescents exhibit self-aggrandizement and arrogance. The increased self-investment also can result in an increased bodily concern, a hypochondriacal worry about their bodily functioning. That is, a preoccupation with early signs of imagined serious illness.

A particularly self-defeating way resorted to fill the void and not feel lonely might be to become gluttonous regarding food. An even more self-defeating enterprise is resorting to drugs. Adolescents often have keen sensitivity to their environment. Many adolescents become keenly aware of the beauty of (Mother) nature. Perhaps resort to hallucinogenic drugs is to make sensory processes, such as vision and hearing, even more sensitive. Is this an attempt at restitution to hold onto the external world populated by parents? Only a few adolescents will experiment with hallucinogenics. Drugs like marijuana, however, are very present in high schools. When used recreationally, and rarely, there seems to be no lasting psychological danger. Used rarely, it seems to not harm the brain or lungs. There is, however, a potential legal consequence. A concern is when the adolescent uses it daily, maybe multiple times. The danger then is it drains initiative in all areas of life. Whether there are permanent neurological or pulmonary consequences is unclear.

Parents can be a resource for their children to talk about drug and alcohol use. Adolescents probably already know the basic facts from school presentations. They will ask parents if at their age they drank and/or used drugs of any kind. As always, I think the truth is called for. Parents can acknowledge that when they were once their child's age they, too, were curious about drugs and subject to peer pressure. Parents need to recognize they are not a witness in a courtroom being cross-examined by their child. Parents have the benefits of experience and a perspective different from their child's peers. If a parent did experiment with a drug I believe that this can be acknowledged as well as how, with hindsight, that an altered consciousness was not all that it was held up to be. Children can be told that pleasure can be experienced while sober and not influenced by drugs. The potential slippery slope of recreational drugs like marijuana and dangers associated with contaminant-laced drugs can be pointed out to them. The health risks of alcohol abuse and the benefits of sobriety can be underscored. The occasional use of moderate amounts of alcohol and wine with food can be distinguished from abuse.

Parents can also be a resource for their children about safety issues with regard to driving a car. Most adolescents have better reflexes than adults. The danger lies in the inclination for the adolescent to take risks. Peer pressure can also play a role. Distractions and lapses in judgment are more likely when there are many adolescents in the car. Parents can set limits and educate an adolescent about the dangers of driving while under the influence of alcohol or drugs. They can be examples of safe driving.

In some instances, an adolescent can become so distraught they make a suicidal gesture or even an attempt. Adolescents may still be operating in an omnipotent way and thinking of themselves as immortal when suicide is considered. Often the depression covers over rage at significant people in their lives, e.g., jealous rage towards a girl or boy who has chosen someone else. If suicidal thoughts are acted out the adolescent and family will need professional help. Often a suicidal gesture is a "call for help."

Many adolescents become defiant and rebellious. Some do not accept compromise. It makes them feel weak and dependent. This is in the context of underlying pulls on them to regress and give into the resurgence of early forms of urges connected to their earlier relationship to mother. They employ defenses that will keep the mother at a distance, e.g., feeling hate in place of love, and directing feelings meant for mother onto other people. A few adolescents resort to asceticism, as a way of controlling all urges. This was more prevalent in previous generations. Some adolescents may use intellectualization, a passionate conviction about the rightness of their position about a social cause or the wrongness of a social injustice, where the personal meaning of it to their life is obscure. In our culture, there is an emphasis on action and materialism. This means that the creative and safe restitution forms open to earlier generations of adolescents, are not "in the radar" of contemporary adolescents, such as keeping a diary or journal. Modern adolescents are members of groups. Group affiliation lends itself to filling some of the inner void. Modern gadgets, allowing for emailing or texting, and the Internet with web sites that allow social networking, such as My Space or Facebook, contributes to satisfying the object hunger of adolescents. While this may be a positive consequence for some adolescents, earlier, in the chapter on Latency, I presented some concerns about virtual or cyberspace reality on children, particularly on adolescents.

Once the adolescent has successfully traversed the rocky terrain of finding a heterosexual love object, the sense of mourning and loneliness is reduced or goes away and the need to seek restitution is diminished. The adolescent is in the throes of "first love." The defusion of loving and hating feelings during the internal detachment from the infantile love objects (parents) can be refused in the attachment to the new love interest. Fusion of erotic and aggressive urges results in a dilution of the aggressiveness. The rebelliousness and defiance of the adolescent often diminishes at this point. The male and female adolescent, may express tender love, respectively, towards a girlfriend or boyfriend. This underscores the lasting value of expressions of tender love by parents towards their young children. The defiant adolescent presumably can express tender love insofar as he or she once felt it.

Adolescents are capable of more complicated forms of thinking compared to their younger counterparts. They are now capable of formal operations, a level of thinking enabling them to be less self-centered and to be more objective. Theorizing is advanced, much different from the theorizing of the four year-old trying to make sense of conception and birth. Abstract thinking is advanced. Thinking now serves trial action. Consequences of actions are thought through in the mind. Hence, overt action tendencies are under better control. Risk-taking diminishes and impulse control increases as the brain matures. Problem solving reaches new heights. Interests and skills insure self-esteem. Thinking is not restricted to the present. The future can now be contemplated, at least sometimes.

Sublimation (and de-aggressivization) is increasingly possible. As described above, this is a process whereby drives have been altered sufficiently from their original sexual or aggressive aims so that the mind need not be on continual defense against their entry into consciousness and/or expression into action. Sublimation is involved in creativity. Adolescents can be very creative. The ability to fantasize and suspend reality testing and to engage in controlled regression is increased so as to enliven the reason of the ego with the magic of the unconscious. Adolescents are more capable to regulate these mental processes. Creativity will express itself in performing arts like dance, music, and theater, as well as in writing. If you have ever gone to a high school theater production, either of a drama or a musical, you know what I mean. Adolescents are some of the most energetic and devoted fighters to correct social injustices. They volunteer at homeless shelters, they assist at animal protection centers, they protest against bigotry and against international violence, etc. This generation of adolescents are much more accepting of divergent life styles and cultures than previous generations.

Sexual intimacy among contemporary adolescents is common. It may involve everything but actual sexual intercourse. Indications are that many young adolescents "hook up," i.e., engage in sex short of intercourse. I doubt that prevalence is greater now than in previous generations. It seems, rather, that it is less hidden. I am not confident as to what most accounts for this observation. Perhaps it is the diminished social taboos in society about sexual expression, adults as models who are less inhibited in dress and behavior, in the diminished importance of the church or synagogue in family life, the risqué display of sex on television and in movies, the increased prevalence of divorce undermining parental authority, the increased awareness and availability of birth control measures, etc.

For many adolescents, sexuality is a scary enterprise. Girls, especially, may attempt to shield themselves from boys noticing them. They may wear baggy sweatshirts. They even may resort to extreme dieting and exercising. This is called anorexia. Binge eating and purging is known as bulimia. Anorexia often is an unconscious attempt to rid the body of feminine contours so a girl will be less physically attractive to boys. An additional meaning is to get out from under the perceived control of mother whom is associated with food. This behavior is provocative insofar as it jeopardizes health, and, if anything, a mother will get concerned and become even more involved in a daughter's life. This belies the overt protest of an adolescent that he or she wants more independence. Unconsciously, the adolescent is conflicted about wishing to be dependent. If a child becomes anorexic, it is prudent to seek professional help. It makes no sense to wait till hospitalization is required to feed an adolescent intravenously. Close contact with a pediatrician or adolescent medicine specialist is a good idea insofar as the health of an anorexic or bulimic child is compromised.

But what is the consequence of sexual experiences for adolescents? It probably depends on the age and maturity of the adolescent, on if the sex was forced or voluntary for both parties, on the frequency, etc. I think males are more inherently promiscuous than females, in general. An adolescent girl more than the boy will likely feel an emotional attachment to her partner. There is a gender difference here, insofar as males are more governed by their libido and females take into account feelings too. This puts a girl in a vulnerable position to experience hurt feelings if it is not mutual. For some adolescents, parental disapproval of adolescent mores will not act as a strong deterrent. Self-regulation is lacking in many adolescents who are sexually active. Some of this group may not have experienced limits as younger children. I believe that lecturing will not constrain adolescents. Hopefully, there will be opportunities for a meaningful conversation.

We need to be clear that when we speak of "sex" what is it that we mean? Does "sex" refer only to intercourse or could it refer to kissing? Parents must decide what they consider acceptable and non-acceptable. I think, more importantly, is the communication that sexual intimacy will cause intense emotional feelings. I think it is a mistake to be untruthful about the pleasure that is part of a sexual experience. Most adolescents, having experienced masturbatory pleasure, will know you are being duplicitous. I suggest letting an adolescent consider that when sexual intimacy is experienced casually, and not in the context of a sustained emotional connection, intense hurtful feelings may result. I encourage linking up sexual intimacy, particularly intercourse, with emotional maturity. It elevates sexual intimacy to something special, an emotional experience in the context of a mutually respectful relationship that can be looked forward to and can prudently be put off to the future. The risk of unwanted pregnancy can be part of this discussion. Also on another occasion, without scaring them, adolescents need to be educated about STDs and HIV. Presumably, these heath issues have already been taught in high school as part of the curriculum on personal hygiene and health. For religiously observant parents, sexual involvement will be linked to marriage and abstinence will be valued.

Masturbation in adolescence is engaged in by both sexes. Actually it starts years earlier but during the adolescent years it is essentially universal. We know there is no physical or psychic harm resulting from this activity. Masturbation helps to integrate the mind and the body; erotic thoughts connect with bodily feelings of desire. Children should not be made to feel ashamed or guilty about the activity. Often they are more ashamed by the accompanying fantasies than by the actual act of masturbation. Here again one should not imply fantasying as shameful. The content of such fantasies change although a central one may be held onto forever. This particular fantasy is valued because it expresses the ultimate imagined pleasure to the person. It is like an erotic signature. Some older adolescent boys masturbate daily. For excessively shy boys there is some concern. This concern is not because of the activity or fantasy *per se*, but because the daily activity may result in a side effect of elevating fantasy to a position superior to the real thing and diminishing interpersonal initiative even more. When masturbation has not attained addictive status, it can beneficially contribute to comfort with aloneness.

Adolescents are now capable of taking over full ownership of their bodies, although by some of their actions, as a parent you might disagree. They still might wear only a tee shirt in cold weather! They need to be given the responsibility of managing their own bodily needs. I'm particularly thinking here of bedtime. If they are tired in the morning because they stayed up late doing homework because they were on the phone too long, then they will learn there are consequences for actions. Adolescents will learn to manage time better because they will understand they need more sleep. It need not be a catastrophic event.

Being a parent of an adolescent can be very trying for reasons already mentioned. I'm thinking particularly of the arrogance, defiance, and uncompromising attitudes of some adolescents. Also, the exclusion of parents from their child's life is difficult. Rejection of parental values or mocking of them in an attempt to humiliate can be hard for a parent. Failures in school are especially difficult for high achieving parents. The most sanguine advice I can give is "stay the course." Parental aims, ultimately, is for their adolescent to self-regulate. Parents can try to process events with their adolescent. Parents are advised to maintain conviction about family values, set limits when the concern is about safety and mete out consequences where warranted, not in an authoritarian manner but in an authoritative one. An adolescent will argue with his parent and try to test their resolve, especially about curfew. Parents best not take the expedient way out. Parents can consider a professional consultation to discuss concerns before a crisis occurs.

Parents can let their adolescent child know they are available if the child wants a perspective different from that of their peers. Parents can show interest in their adolescent's interests. The "silver lining" is that even very difficult adolescents mature. Parents need to listen to their children's gripes and not dismiss them outright. Children may have legitimate complaints and they will value an apology. By doing so a parent sets an example. In the long run, it is better for children to idealize a parent less and value a parent more, including a parent's warts.

Adolescents are in that stage of life when their sexuality and vitality are waxing, while that of their parents is starting to wane. I think parents mostly admire this new maturity in their children, especially if its expression is controlled and thoughtful. But some parents, perhaps unbeknown to themselves, envy and resent their attractive, sensual, vigorous children. This dynamic could intensify as the child progresses through adolescence into young adulthood. This could lead some parents to act competitively in a variety of ways, for example, by dressing in an adolescent fashion or acting "cool" in an adolescent way. In short, in a misguided way they can act more like a peer than a parent. As commented upon earlier, what adolescents need are adults in their lives who can give them a different perspective on the world from that provided by peers.

Chapter 16
Late Adolescence

Adolescence ends with entry into the second decade of life. We consider the period between roughly seventeen or eighteen and twenty to be the late adolescent phase of development. It corresponds with the last year(s) of high school and the first year of college. It is a time of consolidation, or firming up, of the many achievements of adolescence proper.

For most adolescents, a stable and irreversible sexual orientation has been achieved, they are comfortable with their masculinity or femininity and their gender identity as a man or a woman is part of their self-identity. Repudiation of one's bisexuality is not advocated, but rather an acceptance of its presence. A male can recognize traits in himself that may be conventionally assigned to females, e.g., sensitivity, access to feelings, etc., without feeling this is wrong or pathological. A female might like athletics, be assertive, etc., traits conventionally assigned to her male counterparts, without feeling she is disturbed. It used to be accepted that bisexuality had to be expunged if a late adolescent or young adult was to have a normal adult gender identity.

In psychoanalysis we speak of genital primacy. What this means is that all of the early phases of sexual development and their aims have been subordinated to the primary aim of pleasurable sexual intercourse, even if they have not yet experienced it. The earlier aims serve to arouse, as in foreplay, but not to supersede the genital aim. While this is usually the case, if not, the future sexual life of the adolescent may be at risk. In extreme instances a sexual perversion can result.

During this age period, relationships are stable. Friendships and relations with parents are enduring and, hopefully, fulfilling. The internal representations of these significant people are stable. The senior in high school may already have experienced a long-term relationship, or instead dated several different partners. The late adolescent as recently as two generations ago may have found his life's mate. Now this is commonly delayed into the third decade. As a college student the exposure to lots of peers allows for the establishment of friendships that often endure for a lifetime. Women tend to be more inclined than young men to talk about personal things with girlfriends while guys are more inclined to "hang out," do things together with male friends.

Some interests of young children originate in conflict. For example, sexual curiosity could have been a locus of conflict and resolved by displacement into interest in breeding tropical fish and later into an interest in evolutionary biology. When an interest has become free of its origins in conflict, it becomes part of the secondary autonomous sphere of the mind. In late adolescence there is an extension of this sphere of interests that are stable, seemingly resistant to being drawn back into conflict. Some of these interests may be peculiar (idiosyncratic) to the individual. The functions of the ego that are autonomous congenitally (primary autonomous sphere) or from very early on remain so. Characteristic ways of dealing with stress and anxiety are employed to safeguard the integrity of the self (mind). We refer to this typical response to internal and external stressors as the character of the individual. It is meant to be like a "firewall," although it can be breeched. By late adolescence, the idiosyncratic character should be in place in the personality. More or less, the integration of ego ideals or ideal selves will be integrated. For some, this will be delayed until young adulthood.

It is during late adolescence that voting in local, state and national elections becomes legally possible. This is of significance because it coincides with a rise in awareness of the late adolescent to the larger community outside of the nuclear family, circle of friends, high school, church, athletic team, etc. It is important that this awareness begins for the late adolescent insofar as the larger community is a potential resource for re-evaluating his or her values and ideals. The greater acceptance of parents as representatives of the greater community begins this process. In some instances a modification of values could occur, or broadening, or even replacing of them, with such exposure. It is through such experiences and the exposure to new models that the superego and ego ideal can add additional mature figures to emulate. The conscience can become more compassionate.

Parenting issues are a continuation of earlier adolescent ones. What are unique are the preparation for many parents and their children for the separation that will follow when their child goes off to college. This separation is different from others insofar as parents cannot be reassured that parental surrogates like camp counselors will be looking over the shoulders of their child to make sure safety is not an issue. One only hopes that all the prior years of parenting will have helped to inculcate good sound judgment in their child so correct choices are made.

If a child goes to college out of town, which in the States seems to be taken as an inalienable right of youngsters, then there will be the visits to colleges that parent(s) and child can do together. These visits have the potential for good bonding experiences. My own feeling is that some adolescents may not be ready to leave the nest the first year they graduate from high school. If this is so they should not be forced. One may be able to tell if the adolescent procrastinates sending off the applications. A good heart-to-heart conversation might clarify things. If an adolescent stays around home and attends a local college or community college the first year, the adolescent can always transfer. The child can live at home or in a dorm or apartment with other students in the vicinity. Parents often forget that a "late bloomer" can transfer. If a child goes to college out of town, a parent probably can expect home visits every opportunity. This will diminish more each successive year. Many students adjust easily to being away. Some gain weight, partly because of the high carbohydrates served at school, and partly because of feeling homesick and using food symbolically. It is mother who is associated with food. Parents can be available but best not be intrusive. This is a time for a child to be independent and autonomous and responsible for him or herself. Hence, budgeting money may be a new experience. Setting up a child with a checking account or debit card account makes sense.

Many freshmen entering college already know what career they wish to pursue. Many, however, are uncertain. With the array of different academic courses they will be exposed to, and exposure to peers having diverse interests, hopefully, they will emerge by the end of the second year of college with a direction that they would like to pursue. I believe this will contribute to an inner sense of calmness.

In some communities the majority of high school graduates will not be going onto college. This will be a stressful time for them, given the current economic downturn. Jobs will not be plentiful. Some will become apprentice tradesmen; others might be employed on the family farm, while others will be uncertain as to employment. A small minority may look forward to volunteering in the military services.

PART 2

Chapter 17
Young Adulthood

Young adult years begin roughly with the ending of the second decade of life and conclude with the beginning of the third decade. Many late adolescents will graduate from college at approximately this age and enter their young adult years. In some respects, going to college was a moratorium in life regarding many of the life choices that will need to be made upon graduation. For some youngsters who do not go to college many of these decisions may have already been made. Some life choices will be put off, in these contemporary times, until the fourth decade of life, e.g., marriage and parenting. For some, it may be the time for their first job in their chosen occupational interest. For another group it could be a decision to enlist in military service. Often the choice of military service is based on economic necessity such as planning to use veterans' benefits to get further education.

A practical decision is where to live. In the same town you grew up in or a different region of the country? It used to be, several generations earlier, for children to join parents in the same trade, business, or profession. While this still occurs, it seems there are so many more occupational choices that have opened up with modern advances in technology. Young adults nowadays may choose an occupation that did not even exist when their parents were their age.

Some will choose not to go to college, and instead elect to learn technical skills in one of the trades. They will enter apprenticeships upon graduating high school. Others will go to a community college for such training. Not every high school graduate wants or needs to go to college. Our culture, however, at least in urban areas, seems to value going to college while devaluing "blue collar" employment. There often is a dearth of skilled plumbers, carpenters, electricians, etc. These occupations can provide a good and steady income for those who are less interested in academics and more in craftsmanship.

Unfortunately, such work has less status for most people. Nowadays, choosing a serious job my be jeopardized because of a prospective employer's rejection of an applicant because of their earlier adolescent exuberant exhibitionism on social networking Internet sites such as MySpace and Facebook.

For a minority of graduating seniors from college, graduate or professional school will present another challenge and a further postponement of the "real world." As educational opportunities and economic conditions change, a baccalaureate degree today is almost like a high school degree was for my generation. This means that there is a lot of competition to be admitted to such schools. This adds much stress to young adults, as they go about choosing a career.

Assuming sexual orientation has been decided upon and is stable, which is the case among most young adults, dating that began during late adolescence usually now takes place in earnest. The young adult often is ready for an intimate relationship. Object removal, i.e., finding a partner that is non-incestuous, an unconscious process that begins in adolescence, is usually consolidated in young adulthood (see Chapter 14). Replacements for parents are minimally sought after as love-objects. The circumstances under which young men and women now meet have changed. Dating services, Internet's chat rooms and social networking websites like MySpace and Facebook are important features of the culture of contemporary young adults. Having never experienced the Internet as a young adult I cannot speak from direct experience, but I hear from young people about its popularity. Some people actually meet for the first time, while others keep in touch. It is interesting to me that on Facebook people list many details about themselves, their likes and dislikes, so that there is no longer such a thing as a "blind date." Perhaps this is a good thing insofar as compatibility can be pre-determined somewhat, but it does seem to eliminate the excitement of discovery.

In the States there is a trend towards young adults cohabitating, having children, and not marrying. Reasons given for cohabitating are often to test out compatibility, yet such couples seem to be breaking up more than do married couples get divorced. It is not clear why this is happening.

Changes in what is considered masculine and feminine, and in expectations regarding gender roles, effects young adults. Contemporary young adults seem much more comfortable with divergent life styles than was my generation. Gender identity is not as rigid as it was for earlier generations. Young adults also are more accepting of racial differences than previous generations. These changes have been present for a while now, so that most late adolescents entering young adulthood know what to expect. But for some who grew up in more traditional families, there may be some adjustments to be made. For those where this is not something they can accommodate to, it is likely they will search for a more traditional partner. In some religious groups, arrangements approximating arranged marriages exist.

The sexual revolution of the sixties, of course, has reduced inhibitions so that premarital sex is more commonplace these days. For those without religious objections, birth control methods are readily available. But with increased liberties regarding sexual experiences, also come increased exposure to sexually transmitted diseases. Young adults are aware of this and most take precautions, but some take risks. If an unwanted pregnancy occurs abortion is a possibility, assuming a woman has no religious objection to undergoing the procedure. Some women feel very comfortable with a pro-choice viewpoint regarding abortion. For some other women, there may be mixed feelings that can be conscious or denied.

Young adulthood is a time for further consolidation of personality trends that have taken on stability during the late adolescent years. I am thinking here of such internal psychic achievements such as a synthesis of different aspects or components of the personality. When this is very stable there is likely to be less conflict and feelings of self-worth and self-esteem are sustained. Reconciliation with, or better, an affirmation, of parental values takes place via the endorsement of societal institutions.

Parents of young adults are now dealing with adults. Of course, he or she always has the status of being "your child." The nature of the relationship, however, has to be transformed. They must be treated as adults with recognition of their knowledge, strength, reproductive powers, possibly divergent interests and viewpoints on diverse topics, e.g., politics, religion, etc. They may already be more knowledgeable than their parents about various topics. Most parents wish their children to "outdo" them, but this may threaten some parents. For most, it is not so much competition with their child, as much as it is the realization that some of their own goals and aspirations in life have not been achieved and likely will never be reached because of advanced age and circumstances.

It is a mistake for parents to get too much vicarious pleasure from a child's success. What is "too much?" It is too much if a parent's own self esteem hinges on their child's additional successes and drops with failures. A parent should not own a child's success. If a parent take proprietorship of it, a child will sense it and it will feel very hurtful. If a parent gets depressed if a child fails, it can result in planting the seeds of guilt in the child. A child may recognize and appreciate a parent's life experience and ask for advice regarding job or career decisions. A parent best remember it is advice being sought, not a decision.

There may be a minority of young adults who are not sufficiently prepared yet for the "real world." They may move back into the parental home until they "find" himself or herself. Usually, this is temporary. Parents need to remember, they are adults not children even if they are living "under your roof." If a parent treats them like children or failed adults, a parent is looking for trouble. If the stay in the parental home is not temporary, these young adults may need to be encouraged to get professional help. They may be undergoing a prolonged adolescence.

Chapter 18
Homosexuality

Societal attitudes about homosexuality have drastically changed the past twenty years. Same-sex commitments guaranteed to have the same legal rights as marriages between opposite sex partners are accepted by many legal jurisdictions in the United States. It is a current political issue whether or not to allow same-sex marriages. Several states already have such laws. Twenty years ago this would have been unthinkable. Youngsters have been exposed to all sorts of non-traditional families among their school peers. The younger generation appears relatively nonchalant about homosexuality, accepting of it as a divergent choice among some peers and adults. This is not to say that for any individual adolescent who is dealing with bisexual issues that he or she will be immune to conflict. While contemporary society is more tolerant it likely is not much more accepting of homosexuality. It's analogous to being in support of homeless shelters, as long as they are not in your backyard. Bisexuality, while psychologically present in all people, creates conflict universally. It is one of those inner conflicts, like active *vs.* passive, or love *vs.* hate. These kinds of conflicts are unavoidable and result from incompatible inborn aims. This does not mean that an individual cannot find a comfortable solution to an inner conflict.

The view of psychoanalysts about homosexuality has also changed over the years. It used to be that homosexuality always was considered pathological and we were zealous in analyzing it. Now we are more accepting that if a patient is not conflicted about this choice there is no need to pursue it. Some would say, rather, the choice needs to be affirmed when there is a strong inclination held back by concern about social ostracism. Furthermore, many analysts now accept that for some homosexuals it is a normal variation of sexual orientation that is predominantly biologically determined. Transgender attitudes and behavior in both males and females is not immediately pathologized. We know that identifications with both parents are not the exception but the rule. It is also accepted that heterosexuality does not correspond to "normal." There are variations of heterosexuality insofar as it is a compromise formation, too, and some heterosexual orientations include perverse attitudes and behavior.

Commonly younger boys, and girls less so, gravitate predominantly towards peers of the same gender. Many gay men and lesbians will tell you that as very young children they remember feeling different from same sexed peers, instead feeling a greater affinity for opposite sex friends. Boys may have secretly preferred to play with dolls and play "dress up," while girls may have preferred to play with toy guns or throw around a football. As mentioned in Chapter 9, some girls grow up during their latency and adolescent years thinking of themselves as "tomboys." Most of these girls, however, go on to choose a heterosexual orientation after puberty.

Homosexuality as a preferred sexual orientation does not get determined until after puberty. Prior to that, things are in flux and with puberty choices can change. It is much more difficult to be homosexual in our society so one does not make this choice because of life style affinity but, rather, because of compelling sexual attraction. When a young adult who is inclined to become homosexual but has struggled with this decision for years, "coming out" openly can feel very liberating, especially if there is a supportive community of like-minded young adults.

Clearly, there are some homosexual men and lesbian women who have made their sexual orientation choice based on neurotic conflict. Choosing to abandon heterosexuality for homosexuality may be based upon many different reasons. An individual may feel very uncomfortable and seek help. Males may be scared of women's genitals and want to avoid penetration because of castration anxiety. Other males may have had an absent father and an emotionally unavailable mother and in an attempt to get closer with mother totally identify with her, preferring a male as a love object (partner). For others, they retreat from a positive Oedipal position (where father is the rival) and adopt, instead, a negative Oedipal position (where mother is the rival).

In such instances, competitive wishes regarding father create intense castration anxiety and these young men retreat from such impulses. Girls who become lesbians may have had an absent, or cold father, and a very warm embracing mother whom they remain very attached to. Or they may have had a critical and cold mother so they seek to rectify this in a lesbian relationship. Other girls have rejected their female-ness, may envy males and develop defensive contempt for males in general. When the choice is made on the basis of conflict, professional help is warranted.

Some contemporary young adults feel comfortable having sex with both genders. They consider themselves to be bisexual. In some instances they are making a political statement, often one compat-ible with a militant, radical feminist position on relations between the genders. In others, my hunch is that they are acting out a bisexual conflict. If this is the case, some may find that they feel more comfort-able with one gender compared to the other. I doubt that this is a true resolution of the conflict, but more a temporary cessation of it, only to reappear at a future date. I do not believe we have enough clinical experience with this "solution" to know the long-term results of such an early life style decision.

Parents whose children adopt homosexual life styles are most of-ten in conflict about it. This is less so as our society has become more open-minded about it. But it is a divergence from what they grew up with and strange to them. They wonder why is my child rejecting the life style I chose and modeled for them? Are they rejecting me by choosing to become a homosexual? Have I failed them in some way? For some parents, the objection is religion-based. The presence of HIV virus causes contemporary parents also to worry about the future health of a homosexual child.

Once parents can get distance from taking their child's choice as a personal attack on them, I think they can be more supportive of their child. They can help their child by affirming their choice of an orientation that is natural for them, or if it is a conflicted choice they can support their child's seeking professional help to sort out wishes and feelings. In some instances parents may have to mourn a fan-tasy of having grandchildren from that child. However, nowadays, gay couples are adopting and lesbian couples also are adopting or arrange artificial fertilization for one partner. Becoming a grandparent is still possible. When senior citizens gather, they often talk about their children. Parents with a child who is gay or a lesbian are uncertain about a listener's acceptance of such a life style and may worry that their parenting will be judged. It may be that the more they have accepted it and support their child's choice, and can convey this, the more a listener can be put at ease and be more accepting.

Chapter 19
Middle Age

I'm considering the period of middle age between forty and seventy years old. This period of life could be divided up into the working years and the years approaching retirement. The current world economic crisis of this current decade has underscored how essential it is for middle age people to have a proactive appreciation of saving for retirement and a thoughtful plan about investing these savings so they are not subject to severe downturns in the economy. Also, future retirement plans, even if not well formed, may effect many decisions during the earlier middle age years, e.g., location of residence, educational and job goals, etc. Looking to the future does not mean that the present cannot be experienced "in the moment."

What are the developmental issues for these years? There are many life situational outcomes that have psychological correlates. I am thinking of economic and financial issues, career or job decisions, "empty-nest" adjustments, health issues, grand-parenting experiences, marital relationship changes, friendship losses, etc.

It is during these years that men are actively engaged in their work. There are successes and failures. One may get promoted or fired or laid-off. Being a provider has been the traditional role of men forever. It still is the major role, although other gender roles have been added, such as being a hands-on caregiver. Self-esteem may be based on how much money you earn or the title you hold in the corporation or in the academy. Of course, if one loses one's job there are financial repercussions. For some it might mean relocating the family to another area of the country. This involves loss of close contact with friends, or could mean severing ties with various interest groups that one may have served in or volunteered with. For children, a geographical move means the loss of friends and entry into a new school. These changes can be very trying and, on top of every thing else that parents may be dealing with, their child's feelings will need to be attended to. For non-skilled or skilled blue-collar workers a move might mean a loss in seniority. One's inner sense of security will be jeopardized.

In today's world we are bombarded with media promotions of various material things. We seem to believe we need every innovative technological gadget on the market. We seem to want things to happen quickly, so that we trade up for a new computer because it is "faster." Our automobiles have so much horsepower, much of it is never used. The garment industry is always changing styles and convincing us that unless we buy the latest fashion we will be seen as stodgy or old-fashioned. We can keep purchasing because of the introduction of credit cards, an entity that did not exist for my genera-tion's parents. The point that I am getting to is that people do not save money, or as much as they should according to economists. This has implications for retirement, which will follow at the end of being middle-aged.

Young people do not project themselves into the future. Some-one in their forties needs to start a retirement fund. If they do not, as they enter their sixties they will become increasingly insecure about their financial viability after they retire. Of course, the latest world wide financial crisis of 2008 has everyone worried about his or her finan-cial security. Retirement savings have dwindled in amount. This worry affects all social classes. If you are affluent you might worry that you will be unable to maintain the life style you have become accustomed to. If you are a blue-collar worker you may worry about keeping up with mortgage payments or if your employer will drastically reduce health benefits after you retire and before public health benefits are applicable. These concerns all impinge on the sense of wellbeing for the later middle-aged individual.

It is early during the period I am calling "middle age" that a mar-ried couple or even a single person thinks of home ownership. To own a home is part of everyone's dream. Why is home ownership so important in the psychology of adults? Perhaps it is connected to a primordial need for a permanent campsite (fireplace) protected from the weather. I think it also may have to do with a latent fantasy of being the "lord of the manor" or that "my home is my castle." Within the boundaries of your property you are like a king or queen. Outside of your home you are an ordinary "citizen," not a "powerful monarch". Of course, owning a home has many practical financial advantages, too, that I am not focusing upon. For those individuals whose ownership is in jeopardy because of finances their sense of wellbeing will be undermined. If mortgage foreclosure is a possibility, where to relocate is a real practical issue.

Job or career changes may be considered during these years. The older one gets the more difficult it will feel and be to "re-invent" oneself. It is a natural tendency to become more risk-aversive as you get older. I think this is because the future feels less open-ended and if you make a mistake it seems as if there will not be enough time to correct it. During these years the issue of being a "workaholic" is always present. Because of inflation, overtime is attractive and career promotion is always an incentive to work harder. If you have lost money in the stock market you may also work more hours, if you can, in the hope of replenishing the money. I mention this because a consequence is always a cutback on time spent with partners and children. This is an opportunity "lost." As you get older your children may have moved out, but that still leaves your spouse or companion at home.

The so-called "empty nest" affects every one, especially women who traditionally have been the caregivers and fulltime homemakers. Women benefit if they are not working in a career or a job to anticipate the idle time that will become available as their last child leaves home. There are many different opportunities to get involved in to fill the idle time. A woman may choose to return to school to restart a career or retool for a new career. Job opportunities, however, may not be plentiful in the current economic climate. If being a homemaker and parent is essential to a woman's identity, there will need to be some modifications made. Otherwise her sense of self-worth could be diminished. Her husband or companion, perhaps the sole provider up till then, needs to recognize that his spouse will need support and encouragement. If he is a workaholic then the marriage could suffer at this transition point.

When someone middle aged feels that there is little importance to what one does, one feels vulnerable. It is a time when middle-aged people seek compensations for these vulnerabilities. Popularly, this has been termed the "midlife crisis." A compensation might be the purchase of a new house or car, or engaging in an extra-marital affair. It is as if the new car or lover will be a panacea and revitalize you and you will feel young again. This sounds like a cliché because it is. It does not solve anything but is turned to as a solution by many middle-aged men and women. It seems to me that this is an opportune time for a husband and wife, unburdened by the responsibilities of hands-on parenting to re-find each other. If finances allow, then weekends away or travel and vacations can allow the couple to reacquaint them-selves with romance, if it has been neglected. If this can be achieved, then maybe compensations need not be resorted to. Those who are fortunate to have hobbies or talents can turn to these interests with renewed vigor.

As one ages, of course, health usually deteriorates. The potential for a life threatening illness increases. Middle-aged people in relation-ships usually are available to support one another during scary times. There is nothing harder than to face a life-threatening illness alone. If you have been fortunate to have children who are now grown, they and a spouse, friends and relatives, are invaluable during such a period. During this period of the lifespan, there may occur non-life threaten-ing losses such as diminished visual acuity and/or hearing, decreased strength and agility, etc. When people are younger, health is taken for granted. This is the usual feeling, of course, until one is afflicted with a serious illness. A satisfying and fulfilling life, while not fully dependent upon health, is achieved with greater ease if present.

As one moves towards the end of middle age, there are impor-tant losses to deal with. One's own parents likely die during these years and some friends may have had a tragic young death. We have already mentioned mourning of the role of a hands-on parent as one's children leave the nuclear home to seek their fortune. So many losses will make unavoidable a beginning consideration of one's own death. We will talk more about this later in Chapter 21. Loss and the sadness that is felt is a natural feeling. It is part of the healing process and is healthy. There has been, in my judgment, the medicalization of sad-ness, so that it is treated like something pathological and in need of medication. In most instances, mourning of different intensities fitting the particular loss, runs its course and the person feels better again. There is a phenomenon called an anniversary reaction whereupon on the anniversary of a loss, a person will experience sadness, sometimes not linking it with the earlier loss. It's likely the mind's way of reworking the loss once again in an attempt to reduce grief further. The experience of becoming a grandparent will likely begin sometime during the span of ages that we are calling the middle-age period. I will devote Chapter 20 to this role.

Whether or not to retire will become a major issue for those at the end of their middle age. A decision sometimes is made for you by an employer, as is the case for many blue-collar workers, but even for some in the corporate world or in academia where mandatory retirement rules may exist. For those who are self-employed as professionals or free-lancers there are some incentives to retire once pension plans are required to begin to disburse funds. Sometimes, health reasons are decisive factors determining the decision. If you are in good health, both mentally and physically, and enjoy your work, you may decide not to retire. Some people at this point, if it is possible, may decide instead to cut back and continue to work at a reduced schedule.

For some people, retirement is an opportunity to do an entirely different type of work at which they can still earn income. For others, it is an opportunity to have leisure time to engage in activities or interests that they could not find sufficient time for when fully employed. Grandparents might spend more time with grandchildren. Those with wanderlust may travel. Still others may decide to resume playing a musical instrument they have neglected for years. Hobbies can be re-engaged and interests deepened by means of retirement education offered by colleges and universities. For some, it might mean meeting with friends over morning coffee. Obviously, the permutations are endless.

It is a cliché that some men at the age of retirement when asked how they will spend their time say they plan to "drive their wives to distraction." If a husband has been a workaholic and has had no hobbies, a lot of idle time becomes available. If their wife has been a homemaker she has lots of routines she has established. Now, a retired husband expects her to be available to spend more time with him. But it is not so easy. Tension can result. If the marriage is strong, undoubtedly, accommodations are made on both sides.

Engaging in mental activities that are challenging is a sensible plan. Gerontologists tell us that there is data to support the idea that keeping the mind challenged slows down the brain's aging. Reading books, magazines, newspapers, going to lectures, searching the Internet, playing bridge or chess, volunteering to teach youngsters in elementary schools, etc., are the types of activities that will keep minds active to sustain memory efficiency and to forestall senility. It seems to me that the fundamental foundation for a good retirement is health. If you are healthy you have many more options than if you do not. Financial security is another basic ingredient.

What about being a parent to a middle-aged child? Not much direct parenting of middle-aged children occurs. Parent's hope that the earlier investment in parenting that was made is now paying dividends in their child's parenting of their own children. A parent cannot take all the credit, only some, if children are great parents, and nor should you take all the blame if they are inadequate, only some. I hope from my earlier exposition the conclusion has been reached that parenting is a very complicated business. There are many variables and many that are uncontrollable. It usually brings bittersweet pleasure to older parents to observe their own child being a good, maybe better, parent than they ever were. It is bittersweet because such observations will cause regret that they did not do better as a parent. With age, hopefully one may attain wisdom from experience. Sometimes middle-aged children consult their parents about things, sometimes even about parenting.

Chapter 20
Grand-parenthood

Being a grandparent has been described as an opportunity to have fun without responsibility. I am sure about the fun but not about the lack of responsibility. Grandchildren are a grandparent's legacy insofar as they share your DNA and your own parenting of their parents has indirectly been transmitted to them. Undoubtedly, some grandparents are imps of fun, over-indulging and over-stimulating, leaving the parents, their children, to clean up the mess. The majority, however, do not make such a mess. Most grandparents have a fantasy of an ideal grandchild and they wish to see it actualized. Grandparents with adoptive grandchildren will need to deal with some of the same issues as their children, the adoptive parents. I am thinking specifically of mourning the fantasy of biological grandchildren having inherited some of their genetic potential and thereby passing on a legacy.

I suppose there are some grandparents who envy their grown child's vitality when their own is waning. Most admire it, however, and get vicarious pleasure from it. There is great pleasure watching one's own children be parents themselves, especially if they do it well. Sometimes grandparents are put in the position of mediating between their grown adult child and a grandchild. It can come in the form of a direct request from either party or it is strongly implied. The grandparent is viewed and experienced as a neutral figure. Sometimes this can be helpful, but I think the grandparent needs to reaffirm the authority of the grandchild's parent to help the parties reconcile. In some extreme circumstances, grandchildren are sent to live with grandparents because the parents are emotionally unable to parent. Of course, most grandparents take on the responsibility if no other arrangements can be made, but it must be both physically and emotionally very draining. On the one hand, they're dealing with the disappointment of their adult child being unable to be a responsible parent. On the other hand, at advanced age, their stamina is pushed to its limits by needing to look after an active young child or rambunctious adolescent. There are lots of adults who grew up in unfavorable circumstances of poverty and substance abusing parents who are successful and give credit to and pay homage to a grandparent for being there during their childhood.

In better circumstances, grandparents lend a sense of personal origin and belonging when they tell narratives of personal history to grandchildren. The real appreciation of this will not be felt until the grandchildren are late adolescents, a time when family history and one's place in it is in the context of one's place in the larger world.

Grandparents attend their grandchildren's sport events, and school graduation ceremonies and take pride in their emerging skills and talents. For artists and scientists, their creation or discovery will remain and be valued after they die. For most people, however, a grandchild is our hold onto immortality. We value them for themselves, but also for ourselves.

It is a good idea for grandparents to be involved with their grandchildren from an early age. This way they will be important persons in their lives. In contemporary time when grown children live distances apart from their parents it may not be practical to visit often. There is always, telephone and nowadays, Skype, as a way to keep in touch. When grandchildren get older a grandparent can email or text. If practical, having grandchildren come out to visit without their parents is a beneficial way to bond. Taking vacations with grandchildren is another way to bond.

Are grandparents necessary for the progressive development of grandchildren? Is there something unique that only a grandparent can provide? Could another adult, like an aunt or uncle, do for the child whatever it is that grandparents' do? I guess this is an empirical question that likely will never be answered. There are too many variables to control for an experiment. In the view of grandchildren, grandparents are unique insofar as they are their parent's parent. My gut feeling, however, is that grandparents are unique in what they potentially can provide to grandchildren because of the special biological link they feel to them regarding legacy. I wonder, too, about the second chance they are given to "do it right," so to speak. Grandparents could do a better job "parenting" this time. This can be a powerful motivator to show affection, empathy, set appropriate limits, admire, etc. Of course, grand-parenting grandchildren is not the same as parenting insofar as you are a surrogate. Grandchildren may not view their grandparents to have parental authority. Nevertheless, a grandparent has learned hopefully from past mistakes and does not need to repeat them.

Chapter 21
Old Age

I am considering old age to begin at seventy and end at death. I know there are many people out there who fall within this bracket but who do not feel old but are spry, vital and looking forward to the future to realize new goals. This notwithstanding, there can be no denying that the physical body and the mind is in a period of decline for most all people. The rate of decline may vary but it is inevitable. People younger than seventy think of themselves as "getting older" and not as "old." While society's views during the past decade have changed somewhat with medical advances and increased longevity, so that you hear that "sixty is the new fifty," nevertheless people are considered "seniors" as young as fifty. My criterion is the decline of function.

There is an old saying "getting old is not for sissies." I think this is a valid belief if it refers to the plethora of things that start to go wrong with the body and the mind. To mention a few, stamina diminishes, as does strength, recovery from illness and soreness takes longer, short-term memory fails, vision and hearing impairments are frequent, etc. The interactive side effects of medications take their toll in causing imbalance, drowsiness, as well as damage to internal organs of the body. Old people are much more aware about good diet and the need for exercise of the body and the mind. Some would add the soul and spirit too. People are more proactive about their health. Interestingly, while this is so, and longevity has increased, there is still a shortage of medical specialists, geriatricians, for the aged.

In some cultures, such as Eastern ones, the aged or old people are "revered." Ancestors are almost worshipped. This is not true in Western culture. If anything, the opposite is true. Old people are thought of as "over the hill." They are not "hip" or "cool," but instead are believed to be out of touch with modernity. Popular culture with its celebrities are elevated to extreme heights of influence, while the past and history is devalued as passé. What can an old person know that is of value to a young person? After all, they need help programming their cell phone or using the DVD. Perhaps I am putting this too extremely to make a point. There are younger people who display deference and helpfulness to older strangers in public settings.

But the point is many old people who have not been afflicted with senility or Alzheimer's have lots to offer young people, a wealth of experience and often a perspective based on this that is known as wisdom. To accept this about old people is not the same as denial of the general decline that also exists. Nor do I mean to diminish the enormous creative energy of young people.

I am cognizant of the vast repository of knowledge and information that computers and the Internet makes available to us with just a click. Computers are to young people what the radio and books were to the generation of people I am calling old. But what many old people can do that a computer cannot is to engage in self-reflection about their knowledge and frame the experience in a perspective that is uniquely human with feelings. It is this that earlier generations can profit from.

Many old people accept being redundant as true, but a minority knows they have something to offer. These people volunteer their time to schools, join Boards of organizations to contribute their expertise, and even join the Peace Corps. For some who "give in" to the decline, they retreat to communities where only like-minded and like-bodied people can reside, rather than preferring to live among all the generations so as to benefit from new learning. I do not mean to be dismissive of so-called "retirement communities" which can offer multi-enrichment programs, assisted living services to help those who are physically disadvantaged, such as meals, housekeeping, and transportation, along with medical services. For a segment of old people, such communities serve a valuable function.

For some elderly, the loss or decline of some bodily functions can be very disturbing and humiliating. For men, especially, the decline of sexual prowess or interest can make some feel less masculine and even castrated. It seems less so for women in this area, perhaps because being sexual for most women is more than pleasure seeking and being feminine, but, more importantly, also being emotionally intimate with a specific partner. The intimacy can still exist without the sexual accompaniments. Incontinence is not uncommon among older women and in men who have had treatment for prostate cancer. For both genders, but particularly for men, the loss of control over urinary elimination is an embarrassment and can reduce one to feel like a little child. Some men feel less masculine if they wear a pad to absorb the leakage.

Wrinkles and graying hair seem to disturb older women more than men. "Looking their age" is to be avoided. Face lifts, long hair that is bleached or dyed, and clothes made for a younger generation are sought after to deny and disguise aging. Vanity takes over because of the emphasis our Western society places on physical beauty over personality and good sense. Additionally, looking younger supports denial of ultimately dying.

Parenting now can take a complete turnabout in some respects. The parents of old people are long dead. Old people are in some respects "parented" by their grown children. Some find it easier than others to accept this. Some, a small minority, can afford to hire help, like nurses, handymen, drivers, etc. Others who are poor, too many to allow us to be complacent about the problem, do without help and barely scrape by with some assistance from volunteers in service agencies and religious institutions.

If one's own child assists or takes care of one, an old person must accept being dependent and not feel a burden. Most grown children willingly and lovingly provide assistance, feeling they are doing for parents what they provided for them as children. Of course, there are some who resent it and feel it to be a burden and are neglectful of their elderly parents. Government help in terms of health and social welfare programs, has made a great difference in the wellbeing of the elderly.

Of paramount importance is the attitude that an old person has about a life lived and if he or she has come to terms with dying. If one feels that they have been generative in terms of contributing something of value to the world then they will feel accomplished. What may have been contributed need not necessarily be something of high monetary value like a successful business, or intellectually praiseworthy like an invention, novel, or scholarly paper. These accomplishments certainly can serve as a valued legacy. But also can a beautiful perennial garden or a reputation as being decent and honorable, and so on. Another legacy can be the family that you have produced.

Coming to terms with death is something that Mankind has struggled with forever. If you are a religious person and believe in an afterlife or in reincarnation, dying will feel less dreadful. But if you do not have such faith, then existential anxiety may be disturbing. There are, however, many old people who have come to terms with the inevitable and accept it as a fact and part of the cycle of life. They could even think of dying as returning natural matter to the Earth. Imagining a return to Mother Earth is comforting for some.

Hopefully older people can enjoy their remaining years and are able to take pleasure in the job they did as parents. One may not be a rich person, or have acquired properties, or written a book, but one will be leaving behind a legacy that is more valuable, a child and/or grandchild that one has directly or indirectly parented.

PART 3

Chapter 22
Obtaining Professional Help

We all know that in the stewarding of children from infancy to an emancipated young adult there can occur difficulties on the way. Often these developmental hurdles are just that. They look impossible to jump over when first encountered, but after some small mishaps and practice a child vaults over them. A parent can sigh with relief, and it's behind him or her. But there are other hurdles that are not so easily mastered. Some of these hurdles may be ones that a parent unnecessarily put in the path of his or her youngster. I referred to these as developmental interferences in Chapter 8. Some may be universal developmental conflicts (Chapter 8) that are difficult but need to be engaged by child and parents, with the very engagement itself and a successful outcome contributing to progression in development.

While the potential problems discussed in the paragraph above do not need always to be labeled with a diagnostic term, if even after parents speak with friends, grandparents, teachers, etc., and read self-help books, the issues remain and stress is mounting within the family, it can be helpful to seek professional help. Sometimes pediatricians are the first line of professional help about problems with children from birth through adolescence. Nowadays, their training includes behavioral issues. In some instances a child development expert may need to be consulted. My bias about the comprehensiveness of a psychoanalytic perspective leads me to recommend referral of children and adolescents to professionals trained in child analysis or psychodynamic child therapy. A consultation with such a professional may or may not involve a child directly. It may be that a focus on parenting and becoming informed about the particular developmental phase issues facing a child will be sufficient to help ameliorate the potential problem.

Not all psychological conflicts, however, remit in a quick fashion. A positive, adaptive and progressive outcome may require an extended consultation and recommendation for treatment. Some psychoneurotic conditions with their accompanying symptoms (Chapter 8) may require that a child be evaluated directly. Drug and alcohol addiction that appears unremitting also requires professional help. Additionally, delinquency with or without contrition suggests the need for expert professional help. Sudden school failure may also be a sign of serious emotional conflict. A suicidal gesture needs to be taken as a plea for help.

A disposition session, following several with parents, child or adolescent, may include a recommendation that the child or adolescent enter child analysis, being seen usually four or fives times a week, or psychodynamic therapy, being seen less frequently, with the parents being seen together weekly or bi-weekly with or without the child, usually depending on the child's age. Not all consultations with a psychoanalyst lead to a recommendation for psychoanalysis. The frequency of sessions that will be in the best interests of the family and child depends on a number of factors, most importantly, what intensity is best suited for the needs of the child to get a good response. We hope to achieve the goal of relief for the child and parents and progressive development for the child. The expected duration of treatment usually is a question that parents ask. It is a legitimate question but one that is difficult to answer. It is a bit like asking how long would it take to walk from point A to point B. You may know the exact distance but how long it takes to walk the distance depends upon the length of stride of the walker, the ability to maintain that stride, weather conditions, etc., all determinants that you may not know before hand. How long a treatment will need to last, for example, depends on factors such as the degree of motivation of the patient to work in the treatment, the intensity of resistance on the patient's part, how supportive parents are of the treatment, etc.

A child analytic treatment does not aim for perfection. The goals are much more modest. For children and adolescents, the goal is to restart progressive development. When a child or adolescent is dealing with a psychoneurosis they are unable to proceed with development insofar as most of their resources are dealing with the psychological conflicts that led to a psychoneurotic solution in the first place.

Adults seek professional help for many different reasons. Support for troubled adults who confide in family members or friends can include having them consider a consultation with a psychoanalyst or psychodynamic therapist trained to work with adults. Often but not exclusively, they are dissatisfied with their careers or work and with their personal relationships. They may feel unfulfilled, unhappy with life, given to depressed moods or anxiety, etc. Solutions that they have made can be neurotic ones that attempt to reconcile opposing forces of desire, conscience and reality demands. A good consultation with a trained professional may be helpful to articulate and focus in on what it is that they are troubled by and a recommendation can be proposed as to the treatment of choice that will be helpful to them.

I could say much more about psychoanalysis with children, adolescents, and adults. For that matter, a lot could be said about techniques that are informed by psychoanalytic clinical observations and theory, but are less intensive than child analysis or adult psychoanalysis proper. I am thinking of interventions like work with parents or psychodynamic psychotherapy with children, adolescents, or adults. The focus of this book, however, is on "normal" development and not on treatment. Referrals in the United States to qualified psychoanalysts seeing people of all ages can be obtained on the Internet from the Association of Child Analysis and the American Psychoanalytic Association. The International Psychoanalytic Association can be a referral source as well for psychoanalysts practicing in different locations around the world. Additionally, professional societies of psychodynamic therapists are present in the USA and UK. Many Institutes that train psychoanalysts maintain clinics that offer low or reduced fee psychoanalyses for people of all ages by candidates who are in training. Senior analysts closely supervise their work.

Representative List of Topics Discussed in Each Chapter

CHAPTERS

Part 1

1. The decision to have a baby. Conscious and unconscious motives.
2. The newborn. Sleeping arrangements, breast-feeding or bottle-feeding, etc. The oral phase. Self-other differentiation.
3. Psychological issues of infertility, decisions to undergo IVF, having multiples, and issues of adoption. Premature birth, miscarriage, replacement children. Death of a child.
4. Examination of toddlerhood. Issue of separation, the difference between discipline and punishment, etc. The anal & urethral phases. Sado-masochism. Action. Thought as a form of trial action.
5. The preschooler. Tolerating separation, the internal representation of the parent (object constancy), transitional objects, the meaning and value of play for a preschooler, animistic thinking, real/pretend, imaginary companions, and mentalisation, etc. The psychoanalytic model of the mind and mental conflict.
6. Day care and choosing a suitable place for a child. How to help a child adjust.
7. The psychological issues of the Oedipal years. The significance of this universal developmental conflict and its role in

progressive development. The beginning of an internalized conscience with the partial dissolution of the Oedipal Complex. Family romance and rescue fantasies.

8. Psychological disturbances of the early years are reviewed. Subdivisions include developmental interferences (including trauma); sleep problems; separation/attachment problems; toilet mastery; eating problems; learning problems; sibling rivalry; developmental conflicts; psychoneuroses; delinquency; and super-intelligence.

9. The Latency phase (elementary school years) of development is the focus. It's role as a time of consolidation and preparation for puberty. Development of a sense of competency. Mental processes used by the mind to defend against objectionable wishes, etc. Sublimation. Modern technology (e.g.,cell phones) and development is considered.

10. Helping children cope with divorce. Blended families. The arrangements that are in the best interests of children.

11. Sex education, media exposure and after-school enrichment. In each instance these areas are discussed from the point of view of child psychology and the parenting issues that arise.

12. Sexual abuse. The consequences of such an experience upon the development of children. The definition of abuse is expanded from the common one of physical molestation.

13. The Preadolescent phase is examined for boys and girls. Differences between the genders are noted. Tasks for parents to help children through this difficult time period.

14. Early adolescence and the concerns of young teenagers. Tasks of adolescence, namely, finding a non-incestuous love object (object removal) and the second separation-individuation phase.

15. Middle adolescence. The restitutive attempts of adolescents in their efforts to deal with disengagement from parents. The effects upon parents from a defiant child. Sexuality of adolescents.

16. Late adolescence is considered. A time of consolidation. "Genital primacy" is discussed.

Part 2

17. Young adulthood is discussed. The relationship with parents needs to be transformed. Parents need to realize they are dealing with young adults, not young children. Issues of young adulthood, e.g., career considerations, consolidation of character, sexual orientation, etc.
18. Homosexuality is considered. Changing viewpoints of psychoanalysts. The dynamics that may be involved in bisexual conflict are discussed alongside a homosexual orientation based upon biological determinants.
19. Issues of Middle age are discussed. Topics include the "empty nest" syndrome, compensations that are sought to deny aging, approaching retirement, etc.
20. Grandparents and what role they play in the lives of grandchildren are examined. Is there something unique that a grandparent can contribute?
21. The period of Old Age. Issues of waning health and its consequence on the psychology of elderly people is examined. The reversal of roles so that children now take care of parents is considered.

Part 3

22. Seeking a consultation. I try to distinguish between the kinds of problems that may require treatment such as psychodynamic psychotherapy, child or adult psychoanalysis, or parent work.

RECOMMENDED READINGS

Annuals & Periodicals:

Psychoanalytic Study of the Child (PSC), Yale University Press, New Haven & London, Vols 1-65.

Child Analysis, Hanna-Perkins Center for Child Development, Shaker Heights, Ohio, Vols 1-18.

Bulletin of The Hampstead Clinic, 1978-1984; renamed Bulletin of The Anna Freud Centre, 1985-1995.

Journal of the American Psychoanalytic Association – (Search www.pep-web.org for selected articles).

Psychoanalytic Quarterly- (Search www.pep-web.org for selected articles).

Collected Works:

The Writings of Anna Freud, International Universities Press (IUP), Inc., Madison, CT, Vols 1-8, 1936-1980.

The Complete Psychological Works of Sigmund Freud, Standard Edition, Vols 1-23, 1886-1939, Hogarth, London.

Psychoanalytic Theory:

Brenner, C., 1973, An Elementary Textbook of Psychoanalysis, Revised Edition, IUP, Madison, CT.

Brenner, C., 1982, The Mind in Conflict, IUP, Madison, CT.

Erikson, E.H., 1968, Identity: Youth and Crisis, New York: Norton.

Gehrie, M.J., 2011, From Archaic Narcissism to Empathy For The Self. J. Am Psa Assn 59, 313-333.

Hartmann, H. 1964, Essays on Ego Psychology, New York:IUP.

Kohut, H. 1971, The Analysis of the Self: A Systematic Approach to The Psychoanalytic Treatment of Narcissistic Personality Disorders, New York: IUP.

Loewald, H.W., 1980, Papers on Psychoanalysis, Yale Univ. Press, New Haven & London.

Nagera, H., 1966, Early childhood disturbances, the infantile neuroses' and the adult disturbances. Monograph series of the PSC, #2.

Nagera, H. 1968, The concept of ego apparatus in psychoanalysis: including considerations concerning the somatic roots of the ego. PSC, 23: 386-403.

Sandler, J. & Rosenblatt, B., 1962, The concept of the representational world. PSC, 17: 135-145.

Sandler, J. & Nagera, H., 1963, Aspects of the metapsychology of fantasy. PSC, 18: 179-184.

Schur, Max, 1967, The Id and the Regulatory Principles of Mental Functioning, Hogarth, London.

Sterba, Richard F., 1968, Introduction to the Theory of the Libido, 3rd Edition, Robert Brunner, NY.

Childhood:

Abrams, S.,2008, Transformation: Identifying a specific mode of change. Descriptive and conceptual considerations, PSC, 63, 312-320.

Bettelheim, B., 1989, The Uses of Enchantment, Vintage Books, NY.

Coles, R., 1997, The Moral Intelligence of Children, Random House, NY.

Corbett, K., 2009, Boyhoods: Rethinking Masculinities. New Haven, Yale University Press.

Decarie Gouin, T. 1965, Intelligence and Affectivity in Early Childhood, IUP, Madison, CT.

Decarie Gouin, T. 1974, The Infants Reaction to Strangers, IUP, Madison, CT.

Erikson, E., 1963, Childhood and Society, Norton, NY.

Fonagy, P., Gergely, G., Jurist, E., & Target, M., 2002, Affect Regulation, Mentalization, and the Development of the Self, New York: Other Press.

Furman, Erna, 1987, Helping Young Children Grow, IUP, Madison, CT.

Furman, Erna, 1993, Toddlers and Their Mothers, IUP, Madison, CT.

Furman, Erna, 1995, Preschoolers: Questions and Answers. IUP, Madison, CT.

Furman, Erna, 2001, On Being and Having A Mother, IUP, Madison, CT.

Flavell, J.H., 1963, The Developmental Psychology of Jean Piaget, Van Nostrand Co., Inc., Princeton, NJ.

Fraiberg, Selma, 1959, The Magic Years, Scribner's, NY.

Gilmore, Karen, 2011, Pretend Play and Development in Early Childhood (With Implications for the Oedipal Phase), JAmPsaA, 59: 1157-1181.

Greenspan, S.I., & Pollock, G.H., (Eds.), 1981, The Course of Life, Vols 1 & 2, NIMH.

Lax, R.F., Bach, S., Burland, J.A., (Eds), 1980, Rapprochement, Jason Aronson, NY.

Legg, C., and Sherick, I., 1976, The Replacement Child: A developmental tragedy. Some preliminary comments. Child Psychiatry And Human Development, 7.

Litowitz, B.E., 2011, From Dyad to Dialogue: Language and the Early Relationship in American Psychoanalytic Theory, JAmPsaA, 59, 483-507.

Mahler, M. S., Pine, F., & Bergman, A., 1997, The Psychological Birth of the Human Infant, Basic Books, NY.

McDevitt, J.B., & Settlage, C., (Eds),1971, Separation-Individuation, IUP, Madison, CT.

Nelson, K., 2007, Young Minds in Social Worlds: Experience, Meaning, and Memory. Cambridge: Harvard University Press.

Novick, K., & Novick, J., 2010, Emotional Muscle, Xliberis,

Olesker, W., & Lament, C., 2008, Conceptualizing transformations in child and adult analyses. PSC, 63, 273-279.

Olesker, W. 2011, The story of Sam. Continuities and Discontinuities in Development. PSC, 65, 48-78.

Parens, H., & Saul, L.J., 1971, Dependence: A Psychoanalytic Study, IUP, Madison, CT.

Parens, H., 1979, The Development of Aggression in Early Childhood, Jason Aronson, NY & London.

Roiphe,H., & Galenson, E., 1981, Infantile Origins of Sexual Identity, IUP, Madison, CT.

Sherick, I., 1981, The Significance of Pets for Children: Illustrated by a Latency Age Girl's Use of Pets In Her Analysis. PSC, 36, 193-215.

Sherick, I., 1983, Adoption and Disturbed Narcissism: Case Illustration of a Latency Boy. J. Am.Psa.A, 31, 487-513.

Spitz, R.A., 1965, The First Year of Life, IUP, Madison, CT.

Stern, D.N., 1985, The Interpersonal World of the Infant. A View from Psychoanalysis and Developmental Psychology. New York : Basic Books.

Tronick, E., 2003, "Of course all relationships are unique: How co-creative processes generate unique mother-infant and patient-therapist relationships and change other relationships," Psychoanalytic Inquiry, 23: 473-491.

Tyson, R., & Tyson, P., 1990, Psychoanalytic Theories of Development: An Integration, Yale, New Haven & London.

Winnicott, D.W., 1953, Transitional objects and transitional phenomena: a study of the first not-me possession. Int. J. Psychoanal., 34: 89-97.

Winnicott, D.W., 1965, The Maturational Processes and The Facilitating Environment:Studies in theTheory of Emotional Development. London: Karnac: 1990.

Winnicott, D.W., 1971, Playing and Reality. Tavistock: London.

Adolescence:

Barrett, T.F., 2008, Manic defenses against loneliness in adolescence. PSC, 63, 111-136.

Blos, Peter, 1962, On Adolescence, Free Press, NY.

Blos, Peter, 1970, The Young Adolescence, Free Press, NY.

Blos, Peter, 1979, The Adolescent Passage: Developmental Issues, IUP, Madison, CT.

Brockman, David Dean (Ed.), 1984, Late Adolescence: Psychoanalytic Studies. London: Karnac.

Browning, D.L., 2011, Testing Reality During Adolescence: The Contribution of Erikson's Concepts of Fidelity and Developmental Actuality. Psa. Q., LXXX, 555-594.

Deutsch, H., 1967, Selected Problems of Adolescence, Monograph Series of the PSC, Vol.3, IUP, Madison, CT.

Erikson, E., 1963, Childhood and Society, Norton, NY.

Greenspan, S.I., & Pollock, G.H., (Eds.), !981, The Course of Life, Vol.2, NIMH.

Katan, A., 1951, The role of displacement in "agoraphobia." Int. J. Psa., 32, 41-50.

Marcus, I.M. (Ed.), 1975, Masturbation, IUP, Madison, CT.

Adult:

Colarusso, C., 1992, Child & Adult Development, Plenum, NY.

Erikson, E., 1963, Childhood and Society, Norton, NY.

Freud, S. The Complete Psychological Works of Sigmund Freud, Vols, 1-23, 1886-1939, Standard Edition, Hogarth, London.

Greenspan, S.I., & Pollock, G.H., (Eds.), 1981, The Course of Life, Vol.3, NIMH.